Queer Journey

Queer Journey

A Man's Search for Happiness

Dr. Alexis Rodriguez

Writers Club Press

San Jose New York Lincoln Shanghai

Queer Journey
A Man's Search for Happiness

Writers Club Press
an imprint of iUniverse.com, Inc.

For information address:
iUniverse.com, Inc.
5220 S 16th, Ste. 200
Lincoln, NE 68512
www.iuniverse.com

Although this book is non-fiction, the names of characters have been changed to protect their identity. Similiarities in proper names, cities or stories are only coincidential.

ISBN: 0-595-18329-8

Printed in the United States of America

Dedication

I dedicate this book to all gay, lesbian and bisexual men and women that have traveled similar journeys as mine. To the young boys and girls that are in pain from the words and actions of our society. To the men and women who can't seem to find happiness or joy in their lives. To the men and women that have lost everything because of the choices they've made. To my brothers and sisters that have lost their lives to AIDS and are fighting with HIV. To the men and women fighting darkness and ignorance in our society. And to my daughter, Alexa Rae.

Acknowledgements

I would like to take a moment and thank the individuals that have in one way or another influenced my life. Some of these people have given me the love and support that I desperately needed to continue moving forward in my Life Journey. Others gave me the love and support to complete this book. Thank you to all my friends, acquaintances and buddies that have made my life a learning experience. I will never forget you. Thank you Mom and Dad for demonstrating acceptance and love to your son. I couldn't ask for better parents. Thank you Tata (my brother) and his wife for saying, "We will always love you," when you were the first to know. Thank you to my ex-wife for showing me what true and unconditional love is all about. Also, thank you for the lasting memories that I have from our wonderful life together. I am eternally grateful. Thank you Victor, my partner, for encouraging and supporting me while writing this book. Also, thank you for the patience, nurturing and love you've demonstrated for the past several years. I know it wasn't easy. Thank you to my daughter and precious princess, Alexa Rae. I would have never made it if it weren't for you. I continued forward only because I had you to love. Thank you Alexa Rae for opening my eyes and heart to truth, value and honesty. Lastly, Thank you God for EVERYTHING.

Chapter One

It has been a long journey. It was a journey of tears, pains and growth. My journey began twenty-five years ago. I was ten years old. Only recently, I was able to go back in time and retrace my life. I needed to prepare myself emotionally to walk those painful years. For many gay men, our lives have been tormented by overwhelming pain as children, adolescence and adulthood. Some of us have successfully managed to overcome our wounds, but some are still healing.

I was raised in a loving, lower middle class family. My parents were both Cuban immigrants that worked hard to give their two children everything. My Mother was a warm and caring woman. She lacked a formal education, but was brilliant nonetheless when it came to raising her family. My Father was strong, powerful and extremely intelligent. He was not too nurturing, but I was aware of his love. My brother, Tata (his real name is Mike), was my parents pride and joy. He was the jock. Then came me. I was the shy, timid, artistically inclined, but athletically retarded *faggot* son. Of course, I didn't know I was the *faggot*, but Mom and Dad did. My parents knew all along. Parents always know.

I always knew I was different than other boys. I joined the drama club, enjoyed music and the arts. I was the last to be picked as a team player in any sport and *fag* was my nickname. Instead of fishing, guns, and mowing the lawn, I was more interested in cooking, fashion and accompanying my Mother to the beauty parlor. Instead of talking about girls, I would dress in girl's clothes. While other boys were sharing their sexual fantasies, mine were kept secret. This is when it all began. I would pray to take my feelings away and cry myself to sleep. This is when I wanted my life to end. I wanted to feel no more discomfort or pain. I was only ten years old.

A person can't fathom what goes through the mind of a gay child. Every waking moment, I was overwhelmed with guilt. I felt guilt about my dreams, my fantasies, my walk, my voice and my mannerisms. I was ashamed about myself. I tried diligently to change my feelings about boys, but it never happened. The guilt continued to grow until eventually it became pain. I had so much pain that instead of childhood dreams I thought about killing myself. I thought that the end to my pain would be achieved by death.

I became emotionally stronger every year. I was a young soldier headed out to fight a war. The war I was fighting was my own secret pains, torments, anguish and despair. As the young soldier became a man, the secret grew into more pain, anguish and despair. I became a survivor. I learned to lock my secret deep within my soul. However, what I didn't realize was that eventually my secret would surface. Harboring deep within the walls of my body, my secret grew into more pain, anguish and despair later in life.

I was born in Miami, Florida thirty-five years ago. The date was March 5, 1965. Thirty-something years ago, Miami was not the gay Mecca it is today. It was becoming a melting pot for a diversified group of people. In the sixties, Miami became the refuge city for many families fleeing the communist regime in the Republic of Cuba. My parents were one of the lucky individuals to leave their homeland and start a new life in America. Within several years, Miami became a predominantly Hispanic community. The Hispanic culture, language and traditions were blooming everywhere within the city of Miami.

My parents moved several times until finally settling in a quiet and small city named Hialeah. Today, Hialeah is one of the largest and most congested cities within the megalopolis of Miami. Hialeah is famous for horse racing and nothing else. This is where I grew-up.

My Mom commuted several miles to a textile factory where she earned less than minimum wage and my Dad worked at Chevy Automotive as an assembly line worker. They managed to scrape enough money to buy a moderately comfortable house in Hialeah. The home consisted of a small kitchen, small living room, small dining room, three small bedrooms and one very small pink bathroom. However, the house had lots of room for expansion. The neighborhood was quiet and peaceful. Most of the home-owners were young Cuban families with young children. The afternoons were filled with neighborhood boys playing softball and football on the streets and girls playing Hopscotch on the sidewalks. Of course, I played Hopscotch. My best friend was Larry. He was my *queer* neighbor. I must say, he was most effeminate, but that's what drew me to him. Larry had a twin sister, Marie. Their gene pool must have been contaminated with sewer water because Marie was more butch than the toughest boy on the block and Larry should have been the Grand Marshall of the Pride Parade. God definitely played a cruel joke on their parents.

Due to the fact that both my parents worked, my maternal grand-mother was my predominant caregiver. She was truly an angel. It was dif-ficult to communicate with her because of her deafness, but we still had a close bond. She was the only adult that encouraged me to be myself. If I didn't want to play softball, but learn to sew instead, she was my teacher. She was my shaft that supported me during many shaky moments in my life. She was truly an angel. My parents forbade me to play with the twins, Larry and Marie. However, during the day when my grandmother was baby sitting me, I would quietly sneak out the front door and find my way into Larry's yard. I was drawn to Larry like flies to honey. Larry and I would play for endless hours. Usually, we would play with his sister's dolls or play dress-up inside his sister's closet. The fun ended one late afternoon when my Dad drove into the driveway and saw me parading in Larry's yard with a pink umbrella and red high-healed dress-up shoes. Twirling the parasol and swishing my hips, I paraded the yard as if it was a Paris modeling runway.

I can still hear the screams inside my head. While still inside his work van, my Father yelled at me to get home. As I was walking toward my house, my Father was walking towards Larry's home. He banged at the front door until Larry's father opened the green door. As I heard the yelling roars from both men, I turned to witness my Father striking Larry's dad across his face. Then, all hell broke loose and both men were rolling on the cement porch physically striking each other. All I heard was my Dad yelling to the other man, "My son is not *maricon*." I came inside my house horrified. The word *maricon* was used many times during the brawl, but I had no idea what it signified. *It must mean something terribly awful,* I thought. I ran inside my bedroom and retrieved myself from the horrifying scene. Moments later, my Dad ferociously opened my bedroom door. He began to literally beat the crap out of me. Today, his beating would be considered physical abuse. I couldn't understand his anger or the hatred he demonstrated towards me at the time. He continued to strike my face with his closed fist until the steady stream of blows were intercepted by my Mother's screams. I laid on the floor with a bloody nose and bruises throughout my body. My entire body burned from the excruciating pain. Despite the pain from the lashes, I didn't shed a tear. Needless to say, I didn't play with Larry ever again. Larry and his family moved several months later. Larry died at the young age of twenty-two from AIDS. As for Marie, I heard she later married.

My parents used the word *maricon* frequently. I soon understood what the term meant. It signified a man that was not manly. The English synonym would be *faggot, sissy, queer, fudge-packer, homo,* etc. I was shattered knowing that my parents felt this way about me. My parents mission was to make me *straight*. I was discouraged from playing piano, so *they* chose the accordion, which *they* considered more manly. I was told to join the Cub Scouts of America to learn camaraderie with other boys. I was asked to choose a sport I enjoyed. *They* chose soccer. Anything that was remotely *girlish* was eliminated from my life. Even GI Joe dolls were replaced with guns and trucks. It was obvious to them that GI Joe dolls were made for boys. However, when they saw me placing Joe and Steven in the same bed, my parents quickly decided that Joe and Steven were not proper toys for a sexually confused child. My parents continued replacing my toys with more appropriate trinkets. Their mission was endless and not to mention hopeless.

Everyone knew I was different except myself. One early evening, Teresa, my parents' neighbor, telephoned my Mother to ask for a cup of sugar. I was told to deliver the plastic container to Teresa. I walked through the back alley and came to Teresa's house. She had two daughters. One of her daughters, Junyre, was three years my junior. I knocked at the back door and heard Junyre say to her mom that someone was at the door. I remember her mother responding in Spanish, "It's Alex, the neighborhood *maricon*." One cannot imagine the humiliation and shame I felt as I heard those words.

I recall one day that my Father left me at my parents friends' home. I enjoyed for this couple to baby-sit me. I felt comfortable at their home. Besides, the husband was gorgeous. They only had one television, which was in the master bedroom. I would synchronize my cartoons to that of Ramon's shower. You see, after his shower, he would enter his bedroom while I watched Bugs Bunny or some other animated cartoon. He would enter the bedroom wearing only a wet towel wrapped around his waist. Casually, he would remove the towel and slip into his afternoon shorts. The split second between the towel being removed and his shorts being pulled up was enough to give me an erection for an hour. Ramon was in his late thirties. He was tall and well made. His dark and wavy hair blended perfectly with the fur of body hair that surfaced his olive skin. He was indeed a handsome man. I would watch his reflection from the closet mirrored doors as he removed the dampened towel and revealed his nude body. I can still remember his arms, chest, legs and dick. His penis was deeply buried inside a thick fur of pubic hair which made it difficult discerning whether he was circumcised or *uncut*. He made my own cock stir with excitement. I would fantasize about getting close to him. Touching him. Feeling his body on top of mine. I would lose myself in these brief moments of dreams. He never caught me staring nor did he probably care.

However, his wife did. One day, while performing his traditional disrobing ritual, my act of voyeurism was interrupted by his wife. She caught me admiring her husband's cock. She stood at the threshold of the door and watched me staring at her husband's reflection. My eyes were fixed on his crotch, as she entered the room and began to call me *maricon*. I remember she went toward her husband and cupped her hand over his pubic bush protecting his member from my *faggot* eyes. She ordered me out of the bedroom and threatened to tell my Mom and Dad about the incident. When my parents arrived that evening, the news was delivered upon them. I remember overhearing their conversation. My parents were speechless and humiliated about my behavior. I was taken home and the issue was never mentioned. Needless to say, Ramon and his wife never baby-sat me again.

I was young, yet I knew that my behavior was hurting my parents. I would pray to take my homosexual feelings away. I would cry myself to sleep hoping that I would wake up *normal*. It almost seemed that the more I prayed the stronger the feelings became. I was obsessed with boys and men. I didn't understand my feelings, but I knew they were different than other boys. I was only ten years old. Even though I had not reached puberty, I realized I was attracted to other boys. I was anxious to touch and feel another boy or man's dick, but never had the opportunity. However, I didn't have to wait long thereafter. Soon after my tenth birthday, I did more than touch a man's dick.

My parents traditionally would take my brother and I to the beach on weekends during the hot summer months. It was another normal and ordinary Sunday afternoon at the beach when my Dad asked me to add money to the parking meter. He handed me a handful of quarters, dimes and nickels and sent me on my way to the parking lot. I was putting coins into the meter slot when I noticed next to my Father's car an old customized van with the side panel door opened. Inside were four men. They were Hispanic and in their mid to late twenties. They were shirtless and only had on their bathing suits. They were obviously intoxicated. I couldn't stop staring at them. I stared intensely until finally they called me over to their vehicle. I ignored them at first, but then gave in. The eldest man had his dick exposed. I glanced down at his crotch and began to salivate. He was wiggling his semi-hard cock with his right hand and gesturing with his left for me to approach the van. I slowly and cautiously walked around my Dad's car and approached the van's opened door. Firmly, one of the men pulled me inside the van and then I heard the panel door close behind me. Within seconds, four naked men surrounded me with hard cocks in their hands. The eldest pushed my head toward his crotch and ordered me to suck him. My head was pushed from one crotch to another while sucking each and every one of these men. I continued for several minutes until they noticed my own bulging bathing suit. They began to call me *maricon* and soon afterwards my bathing suit was lowered to my ankles. I saw the older man crawl behind me. I felt my butt cheeks open and he spat thick mucous saliva dead center on my hole. He massaged the spit with his fingers and then slowly pierced my ten-year-old hole with several of his digits. He continued to manipulate my hole with his fingers for several minutes while I continued to suck his friend's cocks. He continued to push his fingers in and then pull them out. Rhythmically, he continued. Then, he withdrew his fingers from inside me and I felt more spit hit my hole. He held me with both hands around my waist and pulled me towards him. I felt an intense and sharp pain as his adult penis went inside me. He entered me with severe force. He spat again and pushed farther inside. More spit and deeper inside he pushed. Finally, he was completely in and began to thrust his body towards me. The pain was horrifying. He continued to thrust and pound my young ass. Meanwhile, I never stopped sucking the other three men. I kept mouthing their cocks until one by one ejaculated inside my mouth. They filled my boy stomach with white man juice. Finally, the older man began to moan and finally shot his load inside me. The nightmare was over. They began to laugh and praise each other on their behavior while tears rolled down my cheeks. I was in pain, terrified and mortified at what had occurred. I quickly wiggled my bathing suit passed my ankles then knees and finally covered myself. The door opened and I was let out. I heard the ignition turn and soon the van backed out of the parking space. I was left behind with such fear and terror that I didn't know what to do or whom to tell. I knew that these men had raped me, but in some weird and confusing way, I enjoyed it. It was a paradox. I thought to myself, *How could I have enjoyed something that felt so wrong?* I returned to the beach where my family was preparing our afternoon lunch. My Dad asked me, "What took so long?" I simply ignored his comment and sat on the beach blanket. I was in awe and severe pain from what had occurred. As I was sitting on the blanket, I felt something trickle down my inner thighs. I thought it was blood. Much to my chagrin, it was *cum*. I was only ten-years-old when I got fucked.

The nightmare is still vivid and real even today, several decades afterwards. I never mentioned this incident to anyone. I kept it a secret. These four men (or animals) became my teachers. Several days after the rape incident, I began to stroke my dick as I remembered them doing to their own penises that Sunday afternoon. I began to *spank the monkey* every day for several months. At times, I would *spank* and *spank* until the skin became raw from the excessive friction. Nothing came out from my piss tube until several months later. I continued to manipulate my cock until one day I felt a different sensation. I continued to rub quicker and quicker until without notice a small amount of white jism flowed out. I knew I had accomplished something. I can still remember the sensation and feeling the first time I ejaculated. From that day forward, I was masturbating several times a day.

That same summer another incident occurred. My brother and I were sent on a trip to Walt Disney World with a local church group. The church financed the trip for young boys that were from poor and economically challenged families. My brother and I met the financial criteria and were given the invitation to the Magic Kingdom. The yellow school bus was full of boys between the ages of ten and seventeen. It was noisy and loud, but fun nonetheless. We arrived early Saturday morning and were separated by age groups. Groups consisted of four boys, two older boys to overlook two younger boys. The day at the park was fun. I enjoyed my new weekend friends. I laughed, rode the attractions, ate and behaved like any normal kid behaves at ten-years-old. No one knew my secrets and no one called me names. I was just one of the boys, or so I thought. The evening came to an end at about ten o'clock.

We headed towards the hotel and in the lobby we were given room assignments. The chaperones put two older boys and two younger boys in each room. I was assigned a room with two seventeen-year-old boys and one fourteen-year-old boy. I was ten at the time. I was told to share the bed with one of the older boys, which I didn't mind. He was light skinned and had a small amount of hair on his legs. I remember his thighs and legs as they rubbed against me while we were in bed. The sensation caused my own boyhood to rise. He still had no chest hair, but his armpits demonstrated a black shadow of fuzz. We each got into bed and soon afterwards I was asleep. However, I was soon awakened by the sensation of someone touching my crotch. As I opened my eyes, I saw both older boys in my bed gesturing to be silent. I was startled at first, but quickly gave in to their wishes. One boy grabbed my right hand while the other boy reached for my left. They guided me toward their crotch where I gently stroked their hard cocks. I rubbed their dicks feeling their pubic bush as it brushed up against my moving hand. I kept stroking. I couldn't see their dicks very well, but I felt them big and thick. They stood on each side of me slightly moving their hips every now and then. Occasionally, I would hear a whispering moan. The boy on my right ejaculated first. He shot his load on the carpet. As quickly as he ejaculated, he turned and fell asleep. The other boy took longer. He was less shy. I was able to massage his balls with my free hand. I remember his balls were hairy. He moaned louder than the other boy, but it still consisted of a whimpering whisper. It was dark. It was too dark to see anything. He got closer to me and grabbed the back of my head and pushed it toward his dick. I rejected the offer momentarily, but quickly was swallowing his dick. He face fucked me for several minutes and at one instant, I felt his hand inside my underwear. He reached inside my white briefs and grabbed my swollen cock. He fondled me for several minutes and then he ejaculated inside my mouth. I gagged, but swallowed the whole portion. He reached for his underwear and quickly got into bed. Then swiftly fell asleep. I remained awake for awhile with a myriad of emotions rushing through my body. Eventually, I also fell asleep. Upon awakening the next morning, I realized the sexual incident was not a dream. I leaned over the side of the bed and noticed a spot on the carpet. It was the spot from the first boy when he shot his load.

I became an expert hiding and listening to adult conversations without my parents knowing my whereabouts. I would become so invisible that even in their presence they felt safe to speak about any topic. One of the frequent topics discussed was homosexuality. My parents would not venture into why people were homosexuals or what pain young men and women faced being gay, but instead they had the solutions to convert gay people into straight. In other words, they had the cure to homosexuality. I remember my Dad late one evening saying to another couple at our house, "The way to cure a *maricon* is to heat an iron rod and shove it up their asshole." He continued to say, "That will make anyone straight." Another evening, I recall my Mother saying to a friend, "If I have a gay son or daughter, I will turn my back on them. That will make them think twice before they become gay." She went on to say more stupid statements such as, "Having a gay son or daughter is the most disgusting thing that God can send me. I rather have a whore for a daughter or drug addict for a son then a *dyke* or *fag*." *Wow! I was really in deep shit*, I thought. I had no clue about my sexuality at that time, but I knew that I was certainly different. I was different enough that the comments from my parents were piercing daggers through my heart.

With the exception of my internal pain and torment, my teenage years were as ordinary as any other boy's. I continued to strive at school and music. I achieved Dean's List every semester and earned several awards in music. However, my soul continued to ache from the pain of being a gay teenager. My homoerotic dreams and thoughts were suppressed daily. They were consciously avoided. As I would think about a man or boy, I would quickly readjust my thoughts and feelings to something else. This would continue hourly, daily, weekly, etc. Sometimes, the thoughts were too powerful to control and I felt they were taking me deeper into my boyhood *gayness*.

I was listening to the morning announcements at school when I began to fantasize about Lester. After the endless announcements, we had to stand to salute the flag and pray. I attended a strict Roman Catholic school where it was tradition to pray every morning. As the remainder of the classroom closed their eyes to pray the "Our Father", my eyes were locked on Lester's body. He was my age, but had reached puberty early. From across the classroom, I noticed his forearms had a smooth fur of hair. His face was masculine and his shoulders broad. He stood strong and powerful with his right arm folded across his boyish athletic chest as he saluted the flag. I was lost in fantasy. I began to admire him intensely from across the room. My eyes were locked on him as a lion with his prey. As the morning prayers ended, I heard from the back of the room, "Alex is a *faggot*, Alex is a *faggot*." Rosa continued the taunting until finally she said, "Alex is a *faggot*. He was staring at Lester's butt." I was mortified. I didn't know what to do except to sit and look down at my desk. In unison, the class began to say, "Alex is a *faggot*, Alex is a *faggot*, Alex is a *faggot*." Finally, the teacher took control of the class and made the army of voices stop.

Despite my endless efforts to forget the early morning incident, no one allowed me. I was taunted by remarks every minute of the day. The taunting and name calling continued for weeks and months. The few friends I had were suddenly lost to the legion of vicious sixth graders. Despite the isolation from most of my classmates, I managed to make some friends. They were mostly all girls and were also misfits of the sixth grade society. My girl friends consisted of the ugly, fat and nerds of sixth grade. They had no problems accepting the *fag* into their niche because they were outcasts themselves. I found refuge with these friends. The entire year was hell for me. The comments from the vicious classmates never ended. My priority was not to study my subjects, but to walk as the other boys, to talk like the other boys and to catch a ball like the other boys. No matter how much I tried, I never succeeded to be like the other boys. I continued to walk and talk "funny" and I was never able to catch a ball.

We had Physical Education twice a week in sixth grade. Physical Education is probably the single most frightening experience for any gay child. It was certainly that way for me. The activity of being around other boys playing sports tormented me. The hour of PE was an endless eternity of taunting remarks and laughter from the other boys. I felt I was going out to a battlefield instead of a football field. I remember during team assignments that I was the last to be picked for a team. No one wanted the *fag* in their team and they weren't shy expressing it out loud. Eventually, the humiliation was so intense that I began to have self-inflicted accidents preventing me from participating in Physical Education. I recall one morning putting my Mother's car into neutral gear and pushed the small Toyota forward several inches. As the vehicle moved forward, I placed my hand under the back tire. I repeated this several times until my hand was bruised and swollen. Within the hour, the pain was overwhelming. My intention was to break the bones, but the fracture never occurred. I was excused from Physical Education for one week due to the bruising. The incident that excused me several months from participating in Physical Education was the foot fracture.

Late one evening, I went outside my home and picked up a large cinder block. My Father was constructing a small tool shed and there were several cinder blocks adjacent to the incomplete edifice. I held my right foot in front of my body and threw the cinder block from waist level down on my foot. The pain was intense. I continually did this ten or more times until I fell from the excruciating pain. I lay there several minutes gathering my strength and later stood up. Again, I picked up the cinder block and smashed it down on my foot several more times. I walked inside the house while everyone was busy watching television and crawled into bed. That evening I cried all night from the radiating pain, but I knew it would be several weeks before it was going to heal. In the morning, my right foot was five times the size of the left. My mother asked me what had happened and I simply shrugged my shoulders. I was taken to the hospital where the foot was x-rayed. It was determined that I had several fractures. Again, my Mom asked me how it occurred and I made up a story. A tale only a mother would believe. I was excused from participating in any athletic activities for three months. I was the happiest child despite the pain of my injury. By the time my foot healed, it was winter. During the winter months, Physical Education consisted of cardiovascular exercises and no sports. It was fifty minutes of sit-ups, jumping jacks, push-ups and running laps. Everyone was an equal during winter. No one was a jock and no one was a *faggot*.

Finally, sixth grade came to an end. The summer was a time for me to make plans for next year. I was determined to change my *fag* identity and become "Alex" again. The three months of summer was the dress rehearsal for the coming year. I began to play ball with my brother and master the art of boyhood. I began to date girls outside of my school and by the end of summer I reached manhood. At twelve years old, I had sex with a girl. Ironically, the girl was Rosa. The same girl that called me *faggot* in sixth grade. Her innocence allowed me to take advantage. She was fearful of losing her virginity, but I didn't care. I wanted her to hurt and feel pain as she had caused me. I fucked her once only. That one time was good enough for me. I told my friends about my sexual adventure with Rosa knowing the rumors would quickly spread throughout my new seventh grade classmates. Once again, I would be accepted as a soldier into their vicious army. Those three months were a metamorphosis. My voice, body, and walk were all changing. The outer shell I created was perfect. I was a true man. The inner core was still the *fag*; however, no one needed to look deep inside me. As long as I resembled the rest of the world, my life was perfect. I kept placing layer over layer of armor. Eventually, the layers were so thick, I couldn't see who I was.

Seventh grade was uneventful. I was accepted as one of the boys. I would be consulted about sex and *chicks*. I was definitely *cool*. However, I was burning inside. I had changed outwardly, but inside I was still the same hurting boy. I was once again accepted into the army that once taunted me. Sixth grade was never talk about nor remarked upon. It appeared to me that it had never occurred. Despite my new acceptance and comrades, I was having episodes of depression. The episodes would occur every several months and then go away as unexpectedly as they had arrived only to be haunted by them again and again. During the episodes, I would get home and sleep until the next school day. I remember being angry and bitter at God, my parents and myself. I remember having passive thoughts of suicide. Yet, I didn't know why I felt this way.

My body began to bloom in eighth grade. My bush was becoming thicker. My asshole had a thin layer of fur and my underarms had some fuzz. I was obsessed with comparing my metamorphosis to other boys. However, I couldn't talk about it because the other boys thought that talking about our changing bodies was a gay topic. However, I became friends with Billy. Billy and I would talk for hours and hours on the telephone. We would talk about everything under the sun. One of the topics was in fact body hair. Like myself, Billy was curious about his changing body. I don't know whether Billy was gay or even whether he knew. Billy never had the pleasure to travel the Journey. He died in a fatal automobile accident one week before eighth grade graduation while on his way to a school field trip. The only male friend I had was fatally killed. I was very saddened at his sudden and tragic death. He died in May and soon afterwards I was wearing my graduation gown. Ironically, Billy was buried with his graduation gown. I graduated eighth grade with distinction. I was on the Dean's List and received several awards for my scholastic achievements. The hair follicles continued to sprout and several months later my legs, pubic bush, ass, armpits and face had bloomed into a manly dark brown fur.

Chapter Two

I began to apply to several preparatory high schools. Three schools granted me interviews and finally I chose Pace High School. I was invited to a tour of the campus. A senior student was assigned to take me around and show me the campus buildings and school grounds. It was a half-day of walking in and out of classrooms and buildings. We entered classrooms, laboratories, student lounges, administrative offices and finally the gymnasium. In grammar school, we had no gymnasium or boys locker rooms. We wore our PE shorts and shirts under our uniforms and we changed inside our homeroom. After Physical Education, we would put our uniforms over our sweaty gym shorts and shirts. High school was different. I entered the boy's locker room and my sense of smell was awakened by the humid stench of boy sweat. I looked around and observed rusted lockers where boys would stand alongside naked while changing into their gym clothes. I glanced over and saw rows of showerheads where I would eventually observe naked boys lined-up one after another soaping their bodies. As my student tour guide was commenting about the gymnasium, I was in my own world. I began to obsess with the gym and my own naked body amongst my other classmates. I imagined myself showering and getting an erection. I thought to myself, *What would happen to me? What will the other boys say or do? What rumors will begin to circulate in school?* We continued the tour of the school while my mind was still pondering about the boy's locker room. Finally, it was time to go home. My parents were waiting for me in the parking lot. I sat the entire ride speechless. The gymnasium was taking over my every thought. I continued the pathological obsession and began to feel the pressure of my torments as the day drew nearer to begin my new high school. As the pressure intensified, so did my depression. I couldn't stop thinking about what would happen to me inside the locker room.

In late August 1980, I began high school. During the first week of ninth grade, I recall an intense episode of depression. I was in English Literature when I stood up in class and began to uncontrollably sob. I had no idea why I was crying or the catalyst that caused the crying. Within minutes, I was taken to the counselor's office where we spoke for three hours. The school counselor would ask me why I was depressed, but I had no answer. My parents were called in to take me home. Both my parents arrived with a worried look on their faces. They sat next to me without saying a word. The counselor gave my parents some papers to sign and I was then on my way home. On the drive home, I asked to please refrain from asking me anything about what occurred. I told them that I needed help and I wanted to see a psychologist. The next day my parents took me to my first of many therapists.

The opening statement of my therapist was, "What can I do for you?" I quickly responded, "I think I like boys and I can't continue attending Physical Education. If I don't get out of Physical Education, I will kill myself." I can't remember what the rest of the conversation was about. I remained home from school several days. For the next consecutive days, I continued to visit the psychologist. I realized that my therapist didn't understand the connection between liking boys and being naked among them. I just couldn't tell the therapist that I was afraid of the reaction my body would have while around other naked boys. My last consecutive session with my therapist was on a Friday. I asked him for a doctor's note excusing me from Physical Education. He never gave it to me. On Saturday morning, I searched my Mother's medicine cabinet and found a bottle of *Valiums*. I swallowed a handful of the small white pills with tap water. I was determined to end my life. My plan was to ride my bike to a canal and begin to swim until I fell asleep and drowned. I never swam in the canal, but sat on the bank instead. I sat on the bank of the dirty mucky water all day fighting the drowsiness caused by the pharmacological agents

I ingested. As the drowsiness was taking over my body, I began to get scared. Drugged from the *Valiums*, I walked my bicycle home. I remember falling several times with the bike on the way home. Eventually, I made it. It took me three hours to get home and I was only less than two miles away. When I arrived home, I threw myself in bed fully clothed. On Sunday, I never woke-up. The next two weeks were erased from my memory. I have no recollection of what happened. Several weeks after the unsuccessful suicide attempt, I arrived at school. I was called into the counselor's office where I was told that my Physical Education period was replaced with Study Hall. The replacement was not only for that year, but also for the remainder of High School. I suppose that the unsuccessful suicide attempt made the therapist listen to me.

Ninth grade was a difficult adjustment period. I entered a large school, which had seven hundred students. It was a prep school that demanded many hours of studying and very little social extracurricular activities. If I felt that sixth grade was a legion of vicious soldiers, ninth grade resembled Hitler's army. I had no friends and it was difficult to make new friends. The first several weeks were to establish oneself into a social niche. The jocks migrated together, the pretty girls clumped together and so did every other characteristic group. I was left alone. I didn't join any groups nor made any friends. I was the outsider and the misfit, which chose to be alone. I didn't want to be recognized nor acknowledged. Much to my surprise, the isolation, which protected me, also opened the door to what I feared. I was the token *weirdo* of the class. I couldn't leave my books in my locker afraid the other boys would piss through the vent holes and damage my textbooks and notepads. I had to carry all my books the entire day. I would wrap a thick rubber band around my books that held them in place securely. Despite my attempts to secure the books, they were frequently pushed out of my arms as I ascended the stairwell. The boys that would cause the flights of textbooks and notepads would laugh and gawk. I recall several occasions when I was recovering my books from the floor when ten to fifteen boys around me were laughing, as I quickly gathered them. The hallways were difficult to bear, but so was the inside of the classrooms. One day in Speech class, I was asked to present a talk to the classroom. As I stood up and approach the podium, I heard the murmur from Joe saying, "*Queer* boy on the soap box." The class was in laughter and I in pain. I was the laughing stock of the class and entire school.

I never lacked dates with girls. Regardless whether the gay rumors existed or not, my good looks, decent physique and intelligence were enough for any girl to forget I was the *faggot*. I dated several times a week and enjoyed these girls. It was simply an extracurricular activity. It was a pastime and nothing else. I dated because it was what I was supposed to do. I was intelligent and handsome. A girl's dream come true. I had several dates every week and as much sex as I wanted. All the while, my secret was hidden away from everyone.

It was in tenth grade where I develop a friendship with two boys. Their names were Josue and Oswald. They were very cute and not too bright. However, they were popular and seemed to accept me *conditionally*. We had a synergistic relationship. Their condition was that I needed to do their homework and term papers and in return they would be my friends. We would hang out during and after school. We would go out on weekends and talk on the phone. All I needed to do was their schoolwork. It seemed fair. Josue and Oswald didn't seem too straight; however, I never saw them sucking dicks. We would frequent gay bars and clubs, but they would dance only with girls. The craze at the time was the gay bars. Gay bars were the dance clubs to be seen and they had the best music around. Yeah, right! We've heard that one before. Josue, Oswald and myself would be the three musketeers. We all went out together and slept over each other's homes. Not once did anything sexual happen. Oh, except one time.

We rented a hotel room for July 4th weekend. After drinking all night, we staggered back into our hotel room. Josue, Oswald and myself began to undress. We were drunk and not lucid. Oswald took off his underwear and began to say that he had a big dick. Josue quickly took his underwear off to show his member and it definitely was larger than Oswald's. They both looked at me and I removed my underpants. I was embarrassed due to the fact that my dick was the only one with an erection. Thanks to their stupor and drunken state they never noticed. However, Josue and Oswald soon followed and their cocks began to rise. We all stood around looking at our cocks laughing and giggling. Oswald suggested a jerk-off contest. The winner would be whomever ejaculated the farthest. Josue came in first place and I second. After the jerk-off session, there were three small puddles of thick *cum* on the carpet. I was in awe observing these two boys stroking their dicks. I wanted to reach out and touch their cocks, but I restrained myself from the embarrassment and humiliation I would have possibly caused myself. I wanted their boy juice to spill on me, but it went to waste on the blue commercial carpet instead. I wanted them to act *queer*, yet they never did. The incident was never talked about ever again. They were so intoxicated they probably didn't remember the incident. But, I remembered.

I began to work in a men's clothing store my first semester in high school. It was my first job. I was Dressing/Fitting Room Attendant. That was my actual title. My job consisted of opening fitting rooms for guys to try on clothing. The doors were louvered and through careful maneuvers of my prying eyes, I occasionally would sneak a peak at men in their underwear. Some men wore no underwear, which was a special treat to my eyes. At the end of the evening, I had to clean out the fitting rooms, vacuum and mop the stockroom. The stockroom was a small and cramped room with boxes to be shipped and cartons that were recently delivered to the store. One late evening, while mopping the back room, I came across a *Playgirl* magazine. The magazine was carefully and strategically hidden away behind some boxes. Every evening, I would volunteer to mop the back room allowing myself access to this hidden treasure. The magazine became an obsession with me. I would go back as often as possible getting glimpses of the male nudes. I decided to tear the centerfold and take him home with me. I now had *someone* to admire while masturbating. Every evening the lose pages would enter the bathroom. Then, the centerfold man would *awaken* from the pages to kiss me and penetrate my young hole. Minute's later after ejaculation, the pages would be returned to their hiding place in my bedroom. However, one afternoon, I was running late for work and forgot the *Playgirl* pages in the bathroom. Several hours later, my Mother called me at the store and told me that my Father and she needed to speak to me about something. She sounded very upset which made me worried. When I arrived home and opened my bedroom door, several pages of nude men were laying across the bed. There was yelling and name calling from my Mother and silence from my Father. The pages were torn and thrown away. Again, the incident was never mentioned after that day. I remember falling into a mild depression, but quickly resolved the melancholic state by suppressing the incident deep inside my mind. Within several days, I couldn't even remember what had occurred. I continued forward. I was striving academically, but lingering in self-worth.

In eleventh grade, I was instructed by my English teacher to keep a journal. The journal was not to be reviewed or graded by the teacher. It was simply an exercise in writing. We personalized the cover of the journal with pictures and drawings. Many students' journal cover consisted of hearts and flowers or animals and family pictures. Some boys used cars and fighter jets as their theme while the girls drew hearts and placed stickers on their cover. I was not aware that the only part of the journal exercise that was going to be graded was the uniqueness of our journal covers. My journal cover consisted of a collage. On the cover of the diary was a picture of a large tree. A piece of white cord was glued to a branch of the tree, which went around the neck of a plastic toy soldier. On the top of the cover it read, *"My pain, my secret."* At the bottom of the cover it read, *"No more pain, no more secret."* I was given an "A" for creativity.

I protected the journal as if it was gold. It housed no secrets. It was the only means of allowing my inner-self to express feelings. Not one entry discussed happiness or joy. All my journal entries consisted of the wounds I had encountered and the pain they still were causing. There were endless entries about death, suicide, depression, despair, and many letters to God asking him for help. It is interesting to note that after writing an entry, I would fold the edges of the paper forming a triangle and staple the entry shut. I never went back to read any previous entries. Now, I realize that it was my inner-self trying to come out; however, my outer-self kept it hidden away with staples.

In the beginning of my twelfth grade in high school, a group of guys began to spread a rumor that a *faggot* was going to give blowjobs after school. A group of my friends convinced me to go to the football bleachers after school. There were nine guys not including the *faggot*. This time the *faggot* wasn't me. His name was Alberto. We all took turns sticking our cocks in his mouth. Some of us ejaculated and some didn't. I was one of the few that didn't *cum*. The scene got a little out of control when two guys forced Alberto's school pants down to his ankles. The seniors held him down and the underclassman boys fucked him. Then, it was the senior's turn to fuck Alberto and the underclassman held him in place while he was gang fucked. I stood back in astonishment. I saw the act of violence that was occurring, but did nothing to stop. I was the last guy to penetrate Alberto. As I entered his rectum with my dick, my eyes became wet with tears. I leaned over him and whispered, "I'm so sorry." Once the act of violence was complete, I stayed behind and helped Alberto off his knees. I escorted him back to his car while he cried. Alberto never returned to school.

Once again, I graduated high school with distinction and honors. I began to attend college that same summer. Soon after my first semester in college, I was determined to become a doctor. My major was pre medicine. My secret was hidden even deeper. Everyday that passed my wounds and pain were being pushed farther and farther down. As my pains would float upward to the surface, I would push them deeper to the depth of my soul. I concentrated on my studies entirely. The only thing I had to show was my 4.0 grade point average and seemingly happy facade.

I began to pave my career path. I realized that my retail job was getting me nowhere and began to apply at several local hospitals. I was hired at the county hospital under the title of Executive Secretary/Clerk. I was the Executive Clerk to the administrator of the hospital. His name was Dan. He was a handsome bachelor in his late fifties. He was highly educated, assertive and very articulate. He was quite a catch for any woman, but there was no woman in his life. I once asked a coworker why Dan had never married considering his handsome looks and well-mannered personality. My coworker replied by saying, "He's *queer*." I do recall several instances that I overheard rumors and remarks pertaining to Dan and his lifestyle, but I couldn't believe he was actually gay. It was an eerie feeling to hear such remarks about someone else. Dan seemed neither affected nor concerned by any of these tretorous verbal daggers. He continued to demand respect from everyone and do his job with the utmost professionalism.

Jack frequently visited Dan. He would call Dan several times a day to speak with him. They would carpool together in the morning and have a private lunch in Dan's office mid afternoon. At the end of the workday, Dan and Jack would drive home together. Later, I figured out that Dan and Jack were partners. In other words, they were each other's spouses. They have recently celebrated their 33rd anniversary. I remember that some days at work I would glance at Dan and see myself. As I stared at him, I would see the pain of hiding my life and still harboring my secret sexuality. Despite my admiration for Dan, I didn't want to be him. My goal was to push my pains to such depths that they would never resurface again.

In the winter semester of my second year in college, I met a girl. Maybelle was a senior in High School. She was smart, attractive and articulate. She was a ray of light in my eyes.

Chapter Three

I met Maybelle at Westland Mall. The date was November 20, 1983. I convinced my Mother to join me for some early Christmas shopping. We spent the day in and out of boutiques and department stores shopping for family and friends. We couldn't carry one more bag when I decided to stop to buy gourmet cheese. Despite the crowded store, we noticed each other immediately. She was wearing faded Calvin Klein jeans with a white long-sleeve shirt. She took my breath away. Her distinctive saddened brown eyes, her long hair and her perfect young body were enticing. I was in awe. I would frequently date and fuck girls, but never felt this attraction to another female. She left her customers and approached me. She began to offer me complimentary slices of cheese. After ten minutes of tasting several varieties of cheeses, I agreed to buy a cheese ball. It was a port wine cheddar cheese ball. She took the small box of cheese to the register and began to scan the purchase. I had no cash and needed to write a personal check to pay for the item. I was embarrassed that I had no cash, but it would have been more humiliating not to purchase anything. I made out the check in the amount of $6.39. During the task of writing the personal check, I was wondering how I could ask her on a date. Then it dawned on me. I knew she needed to ask me for my telephone number because my phone was not listed on the check. As she asked me for the telephone information, I smiled at her and said, "Only if you give me yours." After the transaction was complete, she wrote her telephone number on the back of my receipt. With butterflies in my stomach and heart pounding uncontrollably, I went off into the corridors of the mall exhilarated. That's exactly what happened. I couldn't wait to call her at home, so I called her at Hickory Farms. A woman answered the phone and I asked to speak to Maybelle. She answered and I quickly asked her on a date for that same evening. There was silence then a short innocent giggle and then she said, "YES." Plans were made and carried through for my first date with Maybelle.

I drove to her parents' home that Sunday evening. Her mother opened the door and I introduced myself. She led me into the living room where I then had the pleasure of meeting Maybelle's father. Aldo was a strikingly handsome man. His dark skin and overwhelming good looks probably made him a very sought after man in his younger days. He was sitting on his Lazy Boy chair and barely looked up to greet me. I don't think that I made such a good impression on Maybelle's mother either. She wasn't a pretty woman, but had a wonderful figure for a woman her age. She was youthful looking, but lacked the beauty that Maybelle possessed. Dora was brusque and not too pleasant with me. As she let me in, she disappeared into a long hallway. Through the corner of my eyes, I saw her enter the first room on the right. This was Maybelle's room. I heard a muffled conversation between Maybelle and Dora. The conversation was more in the tone of a discussion. Much to my chagrin, their discussion was about me. In a nutshell, Dora made the comment to Maybelle that I looked *weird*. Politely, she was insinuating that I looked gay. Well Mom, you were right! I recall Maybelle during the course of the date bringing up the conversation she had earlier with her mother. I simply looked at Maybelle and began to laugh, giving her the impression Dora's perception was incorrect.

Our date was wonderful. We decided to see a movie at a nearby theater. I can't recall the actual movie we saw, but I am sure Maybelle still remembers the name of the flick. Maybelle must have been so nervous getting dressed that she wore her knit sweater inside out. I discovered the reversed shirt when I was caressing her neck in the movie theater. I came across the designer label and asked her why it was positioned on the outside of the sweater. Maybelle quickly realized that she had accidentally put the shirt backwards and excused herself to the rest room. Upon her return, I noticed she had put the sweater knit inside out AGAIN. We laughed and the sweater remained on her with the label on the outside for the remainder of the movie. After the movie, we went to eat at Denny's Restaurant. We sat in a booth table and spoke for nearly two hours before paying the cashier. Before taking her home, I asked her if she wouldn't mind if I took a detour to a spot I enjoyed. The romantic spot was a remote lake in a small residential neighborhood. We arrived at the lake soon after leaving the restaurant. Maybelle and I began to walk around the lake and decided to sit under a large tree with a very large canopy. The leaves of the large tree were shivering creating a whispering sound of mesmerizing melodies, as the wind would pass through them. Seconds after sitting, I was swallowing her tongue and her mine. Within minutes, my dick was in her mouth and my finger inside her *cunt*. I continued to massage her until she reached an orgasm. It was getting rather late and I needed to take her back home. At Maybelle's door, I gave her a small peck on the lips and asked her if she would consider a second date. We had many, many, many more wonderful dates. Maybelle's mother never seemed to ease her suspicion about her daughter's boyfriend's sexuality.

Maybelle's parents invited me over for Thanksgiving dinner soon after I met them. I didn't make a better impression that day either. I wore a rather flamboyant outfit, which wasn't suitable for Maybelle's parents. The outfit was rather simple, but not manly in any way. I wore very lose fitting pants that tied around the waist with a cord. The pants were a gray cotton material. A tunic shirt was also part of the ensemble. It was a long sleeve shirt made from the same cotton material. The shirt was opened on the front without buttons or clasps. It resembled a robe more than a shirt. A matching sash around my waist closed the shirt. Completing the outfit, I wore gray cloth shoes. I resembled Gandhi rather than an eighteen-year-old American boy. I remember Dora's face as she opened the door. Her face was stone cold, non-expressive and non-welcoming, but she still let me in. She glanced at my outfit from top to bottom several times before reluctantly allowing me to step through the threshold. I was guided to the outside patio where the remainder of the family was sitting and conversing. As I approached the large and noisy crowd of strangers, the loud conversations began to quite down. As the family members began to turn toward me, the conversations seized completely. Finally, everyone was staring at me, as if I was an alien from outer space. Looking at the unfamiliar faces, I couldn't find Maybelle. I stood there in exhibition for several minutes until Maybelle came from behind and put her hands over my eyes and said, "Guess who?" I grabbed her hands and turned around to greet her with a kiss. She said, "You look awesome!" It made no difference what anyone else thought.

My outfits continued to illicit uproar in the family. If I wanted to be a part of Maybelle's life, I needed to alter my fashion statements considerably. I began to slowly change and within several months I was dressing more appropriately according to Aldo and Dora. However, Dora's speculations about my homosexuality never seized.

I remember one Sunday evening Maybelle and I were sitting in her parent's living room watching a movie being broadcast via a cable channel. Her mother for some reason joined us in the living room and we began to watch the movie together. The movie was *Making Love*. It was a film depicting the twisted story of a married man that fell in love with his male doctor. I wanted to change the channel, but Maybelle insisted in watching the movie. I wondered, *Was this movie a sign from God telling me not to continue our relationship?* We continued to watch the movie without a single comment. As the credits were being rolled on the screen, Dora stood from the Lazy Boy chair and without saying goodnight left the room. Soon afterwards, I also stood and gave a good night kiss to Maybelle before heading to my parents' home. I was told several months later that Maybelle's mother was very disturbed after watching *Making Love*. I wanted Maybelle to elaborate further and she did. Basically, Dora told her daughter that the wife in *Making Love* would be her if she married me. In other words, I would eventually leave Maybelle for another man. I couldn't even reply to Maybelle's statement. I was dumbfounded. Unfortunately, Dora was right.

Despite the comments, suggestions and advice given to Maybelle from her parents, our dating continued. At the time, Maybelle was seventeen and I was eighteen. She was a senior in high school and I was just beginning my sophomore year in college. She was brilliant, articulate and beautiful.

For Hispanics, "dating" doesn't exist. Soon after meeting someone (traditionally of the opposite sex), you ask their parents permission to be their *novio* (boyfriend). Becoming a *novio* gives the boy more freedom as well as responsibility. As a *novio*, you can hold your sweethearts hand in front of her parents or give a peck on the lips after your date. However, more importantly, becoming a *novio* entails house visits. This means that you need to visit your girlfriend several times a week. This sounds like any other boy visiting his girl in America. The difference is that you're visiting the family not only your girlfriend. I was told that if I wanted to become Maybelle's *novio* the visits would be three times per week. I agreed and three times per week I was sitting in the living room watching Spanish television programs with Maybelle, Mom, Dad, Grandma, Grandpa and little brother. We were both in school and this allowed us time to separate from the family and study in the dining room table. Sitting across from each other, we would occasionally blow kisses to one another or play *footsy* under the table. I remember seeing her across from me. Her long hair draped over her young face and her eyes covered by thick glasses. She was innocent and so very tender.

After jumping several loops, crossing several hurdles and obstacles and finally earning some acceptance from Dora and Aldo, I was getting bored with Maybelle. Things were going great until December 31, 1983. She was too simple and I was not motivated to continue our relationship. I decided to break it off with her on New Year's Eve. No reason was given to her, no motives and no excuses. I suppose this was God 's way of telling me, "Alex, you're gay!" We were at her house when I gave her the heartbreaking news. She became very emotionally upset.

After our break-up, she became a fatal attraction and would hound me everywhere. She hasn't changed much since our divorce. She would call constantly. She would drive to my usual hangouts. She would follow me everywhere. Then, one day she stopped. Unexplainable, her interest seized completely. For several weeks, I didn't hear from her.

Between January and April, I went out with friends and *partied*. My friends and I knew how to have a good time. We drank plenty of alcohol, did lots of drugs, danced all night in clubs (gay of course!) and had lots of sex. My friends and I would combine alcohol and drugs delivering the most ultimate *high* possible. Eventually, we would end up in very promiscuous sex parties. It made no difference who our sex partners were at these parties. As long as I was getting laid, I was satisfied. I certainly can't recall who was sucking my dick or what hole my dick went inside nor did I care.

Late January 1984, I took a road trip with a group of friends. We rented a van and began to drive north. We spent three weeks on the road sleeping in parks and sometimes inside the vehicle. Nonetheless, we managed to have a great time; however, I realized that my friends were going nowhere in life. My friends were into drugs, sex and nothing else. Out of eight people (including myself) that went on this trip, only three are still alive today. Five of these friends died from AIDS. I began to realize that if I continued to *party* with my friends I would get nowhere. I had too much ambition and goals in my life to throw it all away. I needed to break away from their terrible influences.

In March, I decided on driving to the East Coast with a straight friend. Ricky later became the Best Man at my wedding. Our vacation budget was very tight. We drove Ricky's car northward on this adventure with only a few hundred dollars in our pockets. We had no money to spend on hotels or motels; therefore, we would sneak into hotel swimming pools where we bathed then slept inside the car. We made several city stops along the way from Miami to Hartford, Connecticut. Our first stop was St. Augustine, Florida and then Atlanta, Georgia. Raleigh, North Carolina was next and then, Virginia Beach. We stayed several days in Washington DC until finally arriving at Ricky's sister's home in Hartford, Connecticut.

One late evening while skinny-dipping in a Best Western Hotel swimming pool somewhere in South Carolina, I noticed through the ripples of the water that Ricky had a *hard-on*. It wasn't easy to see due to the darkness of the water. We were standing at the deep end of the pool near a spot light when I noticed the reflection of his hard dick in the motion of the water. Due to the clandestine activity we were partaking in, our conversation was nothing more than a whisper. As our conversation continued, he gradually migrated closer to me. As we continued to talk and sip wine out of the bottle, Ricky continued to move closer. Finally, I felt his hard dick brush up against my inner thighs. I had no intention to move back and kept my position. Slowly, he continued to brush up against me. I suppose he realized that I was enjoying it considering that I was not moving back as he kept brushing his cock on my thigh. I reached toward his dick and grabbed it with my right hand. I began to stroke his cock and felt his left hand lay on top of my head. He pushed me into the chlorinated dark water where I realized he wanted me to give him a blowjob. I did. Coming up for gasps of air every now and then, I continued my activity for several minutes. I then continued to stroke his hard dick until he lightly groaned and I felt short squirts of sperm in my palm. I sat at the edge of the pool and masturbated myself. Hoping he would suck me, I continued. Ricky simply stood at the shallow end of the pool looking at me stroking my cock. I ejaculated and we quickly toweled dried and went inside the car. The incident was never mentioned again. We did lots of drugs and got drunk almost every night during our vacation, but nothing sexual ever happened again. I had a wonderful time. Again, I realized that Ricky was getting nowhere in his life and if I continued my friendship with him, I also would be getting nowhere. I wanted to be someone other than a drunk, drug addict or infected with AIDS.

The time that I spent with my friends was the agent that made me realize what a wonderful person Maybelle was for me. I realized how stupid it was to throw our relationship away. I made a point to win her back.

I finally got my courage and called her on Easter Sunday. Unfortunately, she was at a friend's house. I left a message with her mother. Maybelle called me several hours afterwards. We spoke and decided to meet that same evening. Unexpected and with such short notice, I was not able to buy her a gift for Easter Sunday. Not even a card. Maybelle did. She arrived at my parents' home with a small stuffed bunny and a plaque. Inscribed on the plaque were the words, *"Follow your dreams."* After speaking for several hours, we decided to begin our relationship again. The first obstacle to overcome was her parents. Her parents were convinced that I never cared for their daughter and therefore they were reluctant in allowing me to pursue the relationship with Maybelle again. For several weeks, we were having a clandestine relationship. It wasn't until Dora followed Maybelle one evening and discovered that she was driving to my house. Without suspicion of her mother following her, Maybelle pulled her gray Chrysler Cavalier into my parents' driveway. From my bedroom window, I recognized the white Buick Regal behind Maybelle's car. I needed to be a man and confront her mother. I needed to tell her that I loved her daughter. I invited Dora inside and we sat in the family room where I expressed my true feelings about Maybelle. An hour passed when Dora finally gave her approval for me to continue dating her daughter.

I loved her body, her smell and beauty. We were having sex every day and everywhere. Whenever we met, I was pounding her. I would see her every evening after work. I would take her for a car ride where we sometimes parked and had sex in a secluded lake or park. Usually, we would just drive and Maybelle would give me a blowjob until I ejaculated. Then, I would finger her until she reached orgasm. I remember one afternoon when Maybelle and I had to take her mom to the doctor's office. Maybelle's mom was holding a cup of tea when it accidentally spilled. She opened the glove box and reached for a towel to wipe her face. Maybelle and I looked at each other and began to giggle. Dora was wiping her face with a towel used to clean ourselves after sex. The towel was a white cloth stained and hardened from old *cum*, but it was still adequate enough to wipe Dora's face. It appears that Maybelle and I were always having sex, yet I can't remember one instant that a fantasy of a man entered my mind. I had fallen in love.

In several months, we were going to be separated again. Maybelle was leaving for school in Gainesville, Florida and I was going to Tampa, Florida to pursue my college career. I knew that maintaining a long distant loving relationship was not easy. I didn't want to lose her again. In June of the same year, I asked her to marry me. Surprisingly, she agreed. We spoke to both sets of parents to get their approval. More importantly than our parents' blessings and approvals were their financial support while in school. We couldn't make it through college without their financial help. Both parents agreed that they were willing to help us financially as long as we attended school full-time. Maybelle began to submit the college application to the University of South Florida in Tampa. Within several weeks, she received her acceptance. We would be students at the University of South Florida beginning August 1985.

We both agreed on a date for the marriage. The date was set for August 3, 1985. We had a year and two months to prepare for a budget wedding. Our year of courtship went by too fast to even remember vividly our one-year engagement. During our courtship, we had little money and basically would have inexpensive dates. We still manage finding time to have fun. I remember that every Saturday morning I would arrive early to take Maybelle on an outing. We would drive to a park and sit for hours. We would visit the zoo or simply walk on the sandy beach. Every so often we would give each other a treat and go to the movies or dinner, but never both in the same evening. We simply couldn't afford many luxuries; however, we still had wonderful dates with beautiful memories together. We were two young kids ready and hungry to face the world.

We visited botanical gardens, museums, the county zoo, beaches, hiking trails and the list went on. We always had something to do with each other and always wanted to be with each other. We were both students and had little money to spend on nonessentials, but we always managed to buy something for the day we got married. Whether our purchase was a $15.00 picture frame or $1.00 refrigerator magnet, we took time to choose the right color that suited us perfectly. We took great pride in everything we did for our future.

Despite our financial struggles, we managed to scrape enough money to have the wedding of our choice. We had color coordinated napkins and matchbooks, the finest plastic tablecloths and plastic plates and cups. Each table's centerpiece was a homemade flower arrangement. The bride and groom on the top of the wedding cake were made of resin instead of porcelain. Only the top tier layer of the cake was eatable. The other cake tiers, which were interconnected to one another by an intricate array of flowing colored waterfalls, were made of cardboard and icing. Our honeymoon trip was a gift from my parents. My suit and Maybelle's dress was a gift from her parents. When we finally paid all the debts, we had less than four hundred dollars. With this money, we needed to buy the wedding bands and engagement ring. We shopped everywhere for those rings. When you are on a budget you need to shop. It took us several months to find the perfect ring (or rather, the perfect priced ring). Someone recommended a small jewelry store near my parents' house. They told us that the jewelry was very economically priced and layaway was accepted. Maybelle and I managed to visit the store one late evening. The middle-aged saleswomen demonstrated several rings. However, in our price range there were only two rings. The pleasant women showed us a trio that cost $357.00. Without hesitation, we bought them. This engagement ring and bands were to be used only for special occasions. We decided to purchase two other simple bands with the leftover money. These simple golden bands would be worn daily to school. The more expensive rings were saved for special dinners or special outings. Maybelle never complained about her engagement ring. She was proud of the diamond chip. I caught Maybelle on several occasions holding her hand in the air and modeling the ring for her eyes to see. Of course, she was trying to create a gleam from the diamond, but there was no diamond to produce even the smallest refractive ray of light. It was only a diamond chip, yet she wore that ring with love and pride. She never once mentioned the cheapness of her ring. Several years later, we managed to scrape enough money and I bought her a second ring. I felt that she deserved a real diamond. Her second ring did have a diamond. It was 1/8th of a karat with an inclusion visible to the naked eye.

The year of our courtship was basically deciding about the color of napkins and table decorations. It was a year of extensive planning. Small arguments broke out due to the tension and stress, but they were all resolved. My emotions were like a roller coaster, up and down and side to side. We were trying to juggle a full time school schedule, full time work, wedding arrangements and our relationship. It certainly wasn't easy. We did manage to have many fun times. Every evening before heading out to my car from visiting Maybelle, we would give each other a kiss and a big hug. She would always say, "I love you," just before I walked outside. However, I never once said it back to her. One month before the wedding, after the traditional good-bye and "I love you" statement, I decided to have a talk. We both sat on her parents' sofa and I began to express my concerns. I expressed to her that I was questioning my love for her. Basically, I told her, "I don't know if I love you. I have never loved a person before and don't know *how* I am supposed to love you. Therefore, I don't know whether I love you or not." I remember she cried and then dodged my statement completely. She asked me, "Are we still getting married?" I should have said, *NO* and saved her so much pain but I said, "YES."

I was not only questioning my love for Maybelle, but my mind was beginning to ponder about another issue. The other issue was sex. I began to wonder whether I was suppose to have sex with her every day for the rest of my life. This worried me. I couldn't understand my concern, but it worried me. I have only presently realized that I was acting out the role of a character in a play. I was performing the role of a straight man. I wondered, *What would happen when the production of the play would end and the character didn't exist anymore? Was I supposed to continue the role and have sex?* I wanted direct answers as to how many months or years I had to continue to act out this role. I have always been candid with my Mom and imposed the question to her. Simply, I asked her, "How many times a week do you and Dad have sex?" She laughed and her face turned a pale red hue. She couldn't give me a direct answer and the question was soon swallowed by another topic. I still needed an answer. One evening while visiting Maybelle, I called her mother into the dining room. I asked her if I could impose a personal question that I needed to know. She said, "Yes." I then proceeded with my question, "How many times a week do you have sex with your husband?" She replied with a question, "Why?" I was honest and said, "I am worried that after several months or years my sexual attraction to Maybelle will diminish and I don't know whether that is normal or not." Her reply was enough for me to lay my groundwork for the future. Her answer was, "In the first several months or years, your sexual intercourse is an expression of your love toward your partner. Then, as the years continue, you begin to demonstrate your love in other ways other than sex. You begin to cherish your spouse's company rather than body." This is exactly what I wanted to hear. Now, I had an excuse. If I stopped having sex with Maybelle after several years of marriage, I would tell her it was normal.

Our plans continued forward. Before we knew it, we had August 1983 right around the corner. On the eve of the wedding, I decided to check myself into a small hotel in Miami Beach. Here I could pray, meditate and reflect on the monumental step I was going to take with Maybelle in several hours. I gathered my tuxedo and toiletries and drove east to the hotel in Miami Beach. I checked in on August 2nd. By five o'clock in the morning of August 3, I was anxious to get out of bed. I took a quick cold shower to wake up and headed out to the shore. I wanted to sit there and listen to the waves as they broke at the shoreline. It was still dark and the only thing you could see was the snow-white caps of the waves coming toward the shore. I sat on the sand close to the shoreline listening and reflecting on my life. Several minutes after arriving at shore, a woman by the name of Honey sat next to me. I felt startled at first not knowing where she had come from. I asked her why she was here so early and she replied, "I was sent to be here with you." It was Eerie. The hair follicles on my arms still stand when I tell this story. She asked me what I needed and I simply told her, "A prayer." We held hands and prayed for several minutes looking at the waves in front of us. I lost track of time and before I knew it the sun was rising over the horizon. We continued to talk and I told her about my engagement with Maybelle. Several hours passed, when two beautiful men walked in front of us. As they passed us, Honey asked me, "Are you often *cruised* by men?" I had no remark. Then she added, "That is your life's temptation."

I ask myself, *Who was Honey? Was she an angel sent to me by God? Was she my subconscious talking to me? Was she my gay identity telling me, "What the hell are you doing?"* Or, *Was she simply a homeless and crazy woman walking on the beach that Saturday morning?* Several hours after meeting Honey, I excused myself from our conversation and stood up. I told her it was getting late and I needed to shower and dress. I began to head toward the hotel room. Forgetting to thank and hug Honey, I turned to her. No one was there. I must have walked only five steps before turning around. No one was there. Still today, I wonder, *Who was this lady?* I returned back to my room mid morning and decided on a one-hour nap. After awakening from my sleep, I began to get myself ready for the 3 o'clock wedding. I made it to the church by 2:50 PM.

August 3, 1985 was one of the happiest days of my life. There I stood in a black tail tuxedo awaiting my future wife. I was anxious to see her. The priest escorted me to a small room called the Groom's Room. It was a space no larger than a small bedroom. The decor was simple. There was a comfortable chair in one corner of the room with a two-tier wooden small telephone table next to it. The table had no telephone, but rather a paperback copy of the *King James Bible*. Diagonally from the chair and on the opposite side of the room was a kneeler against the wall with a large metal cross above it. Father Quincy was a young Irish priest that had joined the parish less than a year prior to our wedding. He told me to relax and say a prayer. I couldn't relax and I certainly was in no mood to pray. I kept pacing back and forth as any man would do on the day of his wedding. Shortly after 3 o'clock, Father Quincy came in to tell me the ceremony was ready to begin. I began to sweat profusely. I managed to walk towards the altar. The organist began to play the *wedding march* song and the congregation stood. I turned to face the church's door. My knees were shaking like the leaves on a tree in autumn. It was a bright sunny day and the gleaming sun illuminated the stained glass windows creating a palette of beautiful hues in the church. The two wooden fourteen-foot doors slowly opened allowing a blinding ray of sun to enter the church. I couldn't see her. The bright ray of light in the background created two indistinct figures as they walked toward me. It was Maybelle and her father. I couldn't see her beauty until she was at an arms distance. It was worth the wait. She looked ravishing. She glowed with such beautiful radiance that autumn day. As I approached her and guided her to the altar, her eyes were locked on mine and mine on hers. That was the moment we became one soul. I honestly could have skipped the entire ceremony, I was married to her that instant.

The ceremony was long and hot. Actually, it was boring. After the lengthy one-hour mass, there were the pictures that needed to be taken and the people that needed to be thanked and greeted. I could have skipped this entire part of the ceremony, but I needed to be polite and cordial to our guests. The most important part of the ceremony was my wife. It took about two hours to complete the pictures and thank the guests. Finally, we were in route to the reception hall two hours after the marriage ceremony ended. A white limousine was waiting for us at the entrance of the church. More pictures were taken before we actually got inside the limousine. *Here I am*, I thought to myself, *in a white limousine with my wife*. I was proving everyone wrong. Despite the speculations, I got married. I married not to hide my sexuality, but because I fell in love. Boy, oh boy, was I mistaken.

The reception party was enchanting. The Hall looked fabulous. No one was able to tell this was a budget wedding. In the traditional groom and bride dance, I gave Maybelle a small $30.00 pendant. The pendant read, "#1 WIFE." I looked at her eyes and softly said, "You will always be my number one friend, lover, companion and wife." We visited every table and tried to thank all three hundred guests. For those that we were unable to thank personally, we made an announcement via the loud speaker thanking them for sharing this special day and night with us. We practically danced all night. The hall was reserved until 1:00 o'clock in the morning. By midnight, we began to change from our wedding attire into our departure clothes. Maybelle wore a beautiful bone colored linen dress with a rose colored sash around her waist and rose colored pumps. I wore a black double-breasted suit with a white shirt and a striking red tie. We managed to maneuver through the guests and eventually found our way outside the reception hall only to encounter another mob of guests. As we ran to our blue Toyota Tercel, the guests began to throw the rice. Ricky and my brother decorated the car with inflated condoms of all colors. There were condoms hanging from everywhere and on the back window written with shaving cream someone wrote, JUST MARRIED. We began to drive toward the Hilton Hotel for a much needed relaxing night. The room was breathtaking. It was the deluxe honeymoon suite. It had an overwhelming view of the city of Miami. Maybelle's cousin was the General Manager for the Hilton and was able to get us this particular suite for a nominal price. We were exhausted, but managed to make love. We drank the complimentary champagne and saved the bottle as a lifelong memory. I still have the empty bottle under my sink. Stored away in the farthest corner of the kitchen cabinet, the bottle sits. Before we left to the Port of Miami for the honeymoon cruise to Mexico, we had an early breakfast in bed.

The cruise was great. It was a five-day cruise. The first stop was Key West and then one day at sea. The third day was Cozumel and the next Cancun. We left Cancun late in the evening and arrived on the fifth day back in Miami. We took enough pictures to fill two albums. It was truly a wonderful honeymoon. Even though we were on our honeymoon, we didn't have too much sex. We were unable to make love during the cruise because Maybelle was menstruating. She continued to apologize for the inconvenience and I reassured her that it was not a big deal. Of course not, I was gay. We had a terrific time regardless.

My parents were waiting for us upon our arrival at the Port of Miami. We couldn't wait to get home and show them all the souvenirs we had purchased on our trip. We bought several clay figures, two marble bookends, a traditional Mexican blanket, T-shirts and several pieces of silver jewelry. As we entered my parents' home, there were about one hundred relatives waiting for us. Our relatives and closest friends had organized a farewell party. That was our last day in Miami. We were leaving to Tampa the next morning. I remember Maybelle and I sitting in two chairs in the family room and our family members sitting on the floor around us. We resembled a king and queen surrounded by our court. One by one, we began to open all the wedding gifts. Carefully reading the cards and thanking those that were present when we opened their gifts. It felt like Christmas morning.

A dinnerware set, toaster, electric can opener, rice cooker, slow cooker, pots, pans, vases, ice bucket and picture frames were some of the gifts we opened. Every gift was well appreciated. Late that evening we packed all the gifts into the Toyota Tercel and hitched a six-foot U-haul trailer to the bumper. Inside the metal trailer, we packed our dining room table and chairs, sofa, love seat and bedroom suite. I can't fathom how we managed to put all these belongings into that small space, but we did. We managed to stick every bit of treasure received from our guests into the small hatch back compartment and U-haul trailer. Early the next day, we had breakfast with our immediate family at my parents' home. Then, we said our goodbyes. There was lots of kissing, hugging and a few tears. The scene resembled an intercontinental move instead of a two hundred mile relocation. Maybelle and I got inside our blue Toyota Tercel and drove away waving to our family. We drove north to Tampa, Florida for our first semester at the University of South Florida. The trip should have taken four hours; however, we stopped for a pleasant outdoor lunch in a picnic area. We arrived into Tampa tired, but anxious to begin our new lives together.

Chapter Four

The month prior to our wedding Maybelle and I drove to Tampa in search of apartments. We also needed to resolve certain issues at the university concerning our registration and financial aid. After searching for many hours, we decided on a lovely one-bedroom apartment near the university campus. It was a spacious and airy apartment with lots of natural light coming into every room. The building was a moderately new wooden structure with three floors of apartments. The building had no elevators allowing the top floors to be less expensive than the first and second floor apartments. Due to the expenditure of energy needed to climb three flights of stairs, no one seemed to fancy the second or third floor apartments. Saving thirty dollars per month, Maybelle and I decided to lease the third floor apartment.

We decorated the apartment with hand-me-downs. The dining room table and chairs belonged to Maybelle's aunt. The white Formica and chrome bedroom suite was Maybelle's. The remainder of the furniture was a potpourri of gifts from family and friends. I recall that the most eclectic room was the bathroom. We were given as wedding gifts a red clothes hamper and a blue shower curtain. Then, someone else gave us a green toothbrush holder. We decided to use the spectrum of hues and created a rainbow theme in the small bathroom. The myriad of hues created a palette of electric colors that would wake up anyone in the morning. The apartment walls were white and bare creating an absence of individuality throughout the living space. Without anything to hang or decorate the walls, we used the Mexican throw blanket that was purchased on our honeymoon. We tacked the blanket on the dining room wall and allowed it to drape downward as a French tapestry. Instead of a Victorian scene, the blanket depicted an eagle with Mexican folk art scattered throughout the heavy wool textile. It didn't matched with any other item in the apartment, but we used it anyway as the only wall decoration. Despite the inelegance of the Mexican blanket, it gave us pleasure every time we would sit around the dining room table. We would remember our romantic honeymoon every time we looked at the Mexican cloth. The only furniture that was purchased was the living room suite. We purchased a sofa, love seat and chair for a bargain. It cost us two hundred dollars for the three-piece ensemble. This same living room suite lasted for several years. After the years of ownership, we sold the love seat and chair for one hundred dollars. In spite of the simplicity throughout our apartment, eclectic décor and cheap furniture, we made it our home.

Housekeeping was never a priority especially during the early months of our marriage. Our apartment resembled a teenager's room rather than a grown-ups apartment. Our interests were not to be neat and tidy, but to lie around and cuddle watching television, studying and sex. Sex was the main focus of our lives. We were fucking like rabbits. Luckily, Maybelle was on the contraceptive pill preventing an unexpected pregnancy to occur. Slowly, our relationship grew more and more intense. I recall that in the very beginning of our marriage, Maybelle would sleep on the right side of the bed and I on the left. Within several months, we were spooning from start to finish. Once we discovered the warmth and security of spooning each other, we continued to practice this sleeping technique until the day we separated. Every night and all night long we would be holding each other tightly. Presently, I spoon Victor until we both slip away into dreamland, but for some unexplained reason he wakes up on the right side of the bed and I on the left. Regardless of how much I would like to spoon all night long, it just doesn't happen anymore. Victor complains that spooning prevents comfort while sleeping. I suppose that Maybelle was less selfish about her comfort than Victor. I was noticing that Maybelle and I were going through various stages in our relationship much like her mother suggested would happen. By the way, I'll explain who Victor is later on in the book.

The first stage was a sexual stage in which we couldn't keep our hands off each other and then gradually, the feeling of friendship and companionship entered into our relationship. Sexual intercourse took 2nd place, then 3rd, then 4th and finally it kept moving down the priority totem pole until it was located in last place. We were living Dora's prediction about love and sex. Before I knew it, our relationship was incredibly intertwined that Maybelle and I became one person. I never lost myself in the relationship nor did she. It was a beautiful web of friendship, partnership and love.

Our main responsibility was school. We had no other concerns or worries about life other than to do well academically. However, for some unexplained reason, we needed to share our love with someone or something else. We yearned to have someone or something to nurture, feed and love. Maybelle wanted a baby, but I quickly convinced her on a rodent. We decided to be the adopted parents of a hamster. Maybelle and I named him Tommy. Soon after the adoption of the hamster, we wanted a sibling for Tommy. We purchased a green parakeet and named her after a hurricane that skimmed Tampa Bay several days prior. Her name was Elena. Unfortunately, Elena didn't live to adulthood. She was eaten a year later by our next adopted pet. The next member to join the family was a white and champagne colored Shih Tzu named Faberge. Faberge brought our lives many years of happiness. She was a very sweet dog. It was quite amusing to see Maybelle and I on our frequent road trips to Miami. We would take Tommy, Elena and Faberge to visit their grandparents. After ten years, Faberge was the product of a broken home. I gained custody of Faberge and five years later, I was forced to put her to sleep. She was old and suffering from emphysema and severe arthritis. I remember the day Victor and I took her to the Veterinarian for the lethal injection. It was difficult. She signified a past history of my life that now would perish

The small savings we had didn't last long. We were terrible managing our finances. Our parents would send money for our basic necessities such as rent, electric, telephone and grocery and we would spend the money on

nonessentials such as shopping, entertainment and pet food. We had difficulty keeping afloat with the financial support our parents were giving us.
There was no alternative to our financial hardship, so we decided to get
jobs. We applied at several locations throughout Tampa and finally got
hired at Bush Gardens. I was a games attendant and Maybelle a rides
attendant. It wasn't an easy job especially during the mid summer when
the scorching sun was beating hard and long. Weekdays would be spent
studying and weekends at Busch Gardens theme park. We had no true life
other than work and school. The extra money helped, but wasn't enough.
We had many more expenses and not enough money. We needed to cut
our expenses to the bare minimum. We embraced a frugal lifestyle. The air
conditioner and water heater circuit breakers were shut off on a daily
basis. Light fixture bulbs were replaced by one light bulb and laundry was
done in the bathtub. Despite our frugal attempts, we still needed more
money and I decided to work for a Jewish family as their house servant. I
would work during the week at the Cohen's and on weekends in Busch
Gardens. We finally began to see money in our savings account and the
bills being paid on a timely schedule. I would be in class by eight o'clock
in the morning until late afternoon. After school, I would ride my bike to
the Cohen's where I would cook, clean, vacuum and put the kids to bed. I
would finish between eleven or midnight and then begin the pedal back
home. It was a long ten-mile bike ride. I would arrive an hour later and
shower and begin to study for several hours. It was a difficult time in our
relationship, but I remember these days with such warmth in my heart.
Maybelle also decided to get a second job. She began to work at
Montgomery Ward as a sales person during the weekdays. We juggled two
jobs and a full time school schedule without sacrificing our grades or our
love for each other. In those rare occasions when we both had time
together, we would spend it talking and dreaming about our future. We
would cuddle on our cheap sofa and watch the clandestine cable channels
I had rigged from the adjacent apartment. Though we were very busy, we
never seemed to lose touch with our love for each other.

Our first year at the university was hectic. We worked and studied most of the time. Rarely, did we go to the movies or dinner. Rarely, did we do extracurricular activities. We enjoyed long walks and free concerts on the campus lawn. We received great pleasures spending time at home with ourselves and with our adoptive pets. On Fridays, we would order pizza. We discovered a small pizza restaurant that had a Friday night student special. For ten dollars, we got two medium pizzas, two bottles of sodas and one dozen garlic rolls. It was the highlight of our week. We would eat one pizza on Friday and have leftovers for Saturday night. Our grades continued to be excellent considering our busy schedules. Maybelle and I earned a 4.0 grade point average our first year at USF and made Dean's List as well. Our hard work was definitely paying off. At the end of her second year at USF, Maybelle decided to change her major. After researching several majors and careers, she decided on Social Work.

Where most couple's honeymoon period last six months, ours lasted well into the year. I recall having sex two or three times a day. Yes, a day. Our intimacy did dwindle when we decided for Maybelle to discontinue the contraceptive pill. Eliminating the daily pharmacological dosage, created no spontaneity in our sex life. We were practicing the withdrawal method, which created messier results and more worry. Even though our sexual intimacy diminished, I can't remember ever having sexual fantasies about other men during self-masturbation or during sexual intercourse with Maybelle.

Maybelle and I decided not to take a break during the summer months. We registered for a full academic course load in the summer semester. We decided to take Calculus I and several other electives together. I soon realized her competitive nature. She would study harder and longer simply to earn a better test score than me. Despite her secret competitiveness, we continued to be best friends and incredible lovers.

1986, my last academic year at USF, was very busy. I began to apply to medical schools early in the summer. Maybelle, on the other hand, was applying at other schools located in the same city that my prospective medical schools were situated. We both began to submit the tedious applications and essays early mid summer. By early fall, I received my first acceptance letter to Boston. I applied at six schools across the nation and was accepted at five.

I remember that early fall day when I received my first acceptance letter. Maybelle and I were waiting with great anticipation for the postal carrier to arrive. After several minutes of waiting beside the mailboxes, the postal truck arrived. He began to stuff the mailboxes from behind the metal enclosed box. Diligently, he stuffed letters and fliers for several minutes while we waited patiently. When the stone-faced mail carrier closed the back panel, we opened our small mailbox cubicle. Fingering through various bills and flyers, we finally came to the envelope from Boston University. I asked Maybelle to open the envelope and told her not to read it aloud. She only followed the first part of my directions. She opened the sealed envelope and began to read the content of the letter out loud. She took a long sigh and with a nervous tone began to read, "Dear Mr. Rodriguez: Congratulations on..." That was enough for us to begin screaming with joy. We began to jump uncontrollably as if we had won the state lotto jackpot. I felt great joy sharing this special moment with her. She genuinely felt my joy and happiness. I was finally accepted into a graduate program. Soon after my acceptance letter, Maybelle received her letter of acceptance to Suffox College, also in Boston. We began to make plans for our move to Boston the following year. We still needed to complete our last year at the University of South Florida before our new relocation adventure. My senior year at USF was not difficult. I carefully planned my courses at USF allowing the last year to be relatively easy.

Boston was soon our next move. It was an expensive city and tuition was ten times that of USF. We needed further budgeting and decided to move to a less expensive apartment. We chose Kenmore Apartments. The rent was half of the amount we were currently paying and utilities were included in the base monthly rent. The roaches, ants and spiders were also included with the base rent. It was a horrible looking apartment. As if all the insects weren't enough, we acquired rats as well. One afternoon while watching television in the living room, Maybelle noticed a long wiry object draping over the sofa arm. As she approached the questionable object, she discovered it was the long tail of a rat. We were living with rats! We both were disgusted and telephoned our landlord. Our slumlord accommodated us in a motel for several nights while the apartment was exterminated. We later discovered that these rodents gnawed many of our shoes, storage boxes and ate our food. We had about twelve months to save as much money as possible. I decided to get another job at a doctor's office working three hours a day. After working at Dr. Kien's office, I would ride my bicycle to the Cohen's. Our hard work was paying off. We were saving lots of money for our move to Boston.

I was in a lecture hall during my Physics II class when several rows in front of me I noticed a familiar face. His name was Gary. I approached him after class and began to talk to the familiar face. Several years ago, we were buddies in high school. Unfortunately, we lost track of each other when we left for college. I hadn't seen him for several years. He looked different. Gary was not particularly handsome, but he certainly had something that was attractive. His hair was thinning and completely absent of follicles on the top of his head. He didn't dress elegantly or sharp, but frumpily and tired looking. Yet, he had something. He had a handsome body and beautiful blue eyes. His voice was his asset. He had a soft and sexy monotone that got anyone's undivided attention. He gave people a sense of tranquility as he engaged in conversation. He was also very hairy. We exchanged phone numbers and made plans to get together. Several days afterwards, Gary called me at home and we made plans to go out dancing. He came over our apartment where I introduced him to Maybelle and he introduced us to his girlfriend, Ileana. We began a close friendship and soon Gary and I were inseparable buddies again.

Gary and Ileana lived on campus. The student housing regulations were very strict and did not allow any overnight guests, especially of the opposite sex. Therefore, Gary would bring his girlfriend over on Fridays and stay for the remainder of the weekend. Ileana was a beautiful girl. She was too pretty for Gary. Despite her beauty, I knew Gary wasn't in love with her. His heart was reserved for someone else. It took me several months before I realized that Gary was secretively in love with Maybelle. One day, I asked Maybelle if she found Gary handsome. She replied, "He has something that is attractive, but I don't find him handsome." Her comment was enough to put me at ease. However, I remained attentive at every move he made and every word he spoke. I was jealous for the first time in our relationship.

My last year at USF continued without much excitement. Maybelle and I continued with our plans to move to Boston. In May 1987, we both graduated from USF. I earned a Bachelor degree in Microbiology and Maybelle an Associate degree in Arts. We both decided not to attend graduation ceremony because we didn't want to inconvenience our parents in attending a boring and laborious ceremony. Not to mention, that the graduation ceremony was in English and neither of our parents spoke or understood the language.

We started collecting boxes and packing material and began to put our home into moving status. In early June 1987, I received an acceptance letter from Indiana University. Our hearts were set on Boston when we received the letter from Indiana University; however, IU was offering me a substantial academic scholarship to attend their program. We didn't give it much thought and changed all plans to move to Bloomington, Indiana in August 1987.

In the summer of 1987, Maybelle suffered a devastating accident. The media calls it a *smash and grab robbery*. For those that are not familiar with the Miami crime terminology, a thief smashes a car window with a rock (in Maybelle's case, it was a cinder block) and knocks the victim unconscious. Then, the thief grabs the victim's purse or other valuables and runs; hence the term *smash and grab robbery*. She was inside her Mother's automobile when out of nowhere a young man threw a cinder block through the passenger window. The large cinder block went through the back window and into Maybelle's right side of her head. The impact left her unconscious. Rescue and medical emergency team was notified immediately. She was transferred to the hospital and for several hours underwent plastic surgery on the right side of her face. The blow of the masonry block severed a significant nerve branch that innervated her eyelids, cheek muscles and the lateral movement of her mouth. The blow also severed her salivary duct. I was not informed of the tragic accident until nine hours afterwards. I was shopping on the other side of town with my parents and was inaccessible. When I arrived home, my brother gave me the disturbing news. I immediately drove to my wife's bedside where she was recovering from the operation. Her face was bandaged and her head swollen twice the normal size. Her right eye was swollen shut and the left eye was only half opened. She was incoherent due to the medications, but when she heard my voice she began to overcome her stupor. She held out her hand in search for me. I held her hand tightly. She began to open her left eye and I saw the lake of tears pooling on her lower lid. I was relieved she was alive. The accident made me realize how much I loved her and how much she was a part of my own existence. We decided to stay the entire summer in Miami allowing her to reach a full recovery before heading north to Indiana.

It was mid August, several weeks after Maybelle's accident, when we arrived in Tampa. Our parents joined us on our trip helping us for our move to Bloomington, Indiana. Early morning, on August 18, 1987, we said our final farewells to our family. We hugged, kissed and cried knowing that this move was farther away and our visits were not going to be as frequent. It was no longer a four-hour car trip to visit our family. Indiana was airline distance away. Our parents knew that they would see us once or twice a year, if that much.

We arrived in Bloomington, Indiana on August 19, 1987. The U-haul truck, Toyota Tercel, Faberge and Tommy, the hamster, (Elena was dead by now), Maybelle and myself arrived to our new destination twenty hours after departing Tampa. We were exhausted. I remember we went to the rental office where we obtained the key to the apartment. We walked inside our apartment and collapsed on the carpet. We slept until the next morning. Early the next morning, we began to unload the truck. There was no help around and all the hauling and carrying upstairs was done by Maybelle and I. We finished twelve hours later. We ordered pizza and then collapsed on the carpet. We slept until morning. Slowly, the apartment was becoming a home. Every passing day, the bare walls were becoming filled with artwork, the floor with plants and the windows with valences and curtains. It took several days to complete, but it became a beautiful home.

The apartment was adorable. The building was a white brick, colonial-style edifice. Our apartment was a second floor apartment, but the door to the actual apartment was downstairs. In other words, our guests would come into the apartment from the bottom floor where they would encounter a stairwell leading to our living space. At the top landing, an iron gate separated the stairs from the living area. The living room was large and sunny. Our view from the living room window was the swimming pool. The kitchen cabinets were natural wood, which were in excellent condition. Not too strategically located, was the bathroom located in the same area as the kitchen. The bedroom was last and overlooked the carport and a small forest. We did manage to change the decor between Tampa and Indiana. Thank goodness! Actually, most of the furniture was sold in Tampa. We sold the dining room table and chairs and Maybelle's bedroom suite. We sold everything except the living room sofa. The theme of our décor was *country* and the color of choice was slate blue. Everything in the apartment had some shade of blue in it or around it. After several weeks of hard work, the apartment became a showcased home for *Country Living* magazine. Not really, but we thought so anyways.

We had several weeks before school started and had many days to explore the wonders of Bloomington. It was certainly a beautiful town. We arrived late August and had the opportunity to experience the picturesque color changes of the fall foliage. We would walk through forests hearing the crackling of dried leaves beneath our feet. We would snuggle up drinking a cup of coffee, hot cocoa or warm apple cider on a park bench in the afternoon while the glowing radiance of reds, yellows and amber autumn shades illuminated our surrounding. Sometimes, we would walk downtown and eat ice cream. It was such a heavenly place. I remember us then and I see us now. *What ever happened to us?*

My first year was tough. Actually, it was incredibly difficult. I managed to pass all my courses with B's and C's. There were times that I thought I was not going to make it. Graduate school is much different then undergraduate. It didn't take me long to recognize the difference. I didn't have much time to do anything except study. Even though Maybelle and I didn't work, we were very busy struggling with school. In those rare instances that we would find several hours to relax, we explored the county park. Brown County Park is one of the most ravishing parks I have ever seen. Actually, it ranks fourth or fifth in the nation for the foliage colors in the fall. We would go and have picnics and walk through the natural and untouched beauty of the forest. On occasions, we would camp overnight at several park locations giving us much needed relaxation. We always chose primitive campsites securing our seclusion from the rest of the world. We would arrive Friday evenings and depart from our camping adventure on Sunday afternoon. It gave us a temporary respite from school. I recall these memories with such joy and happiness still today.

Unfortunately, our time spent in Indiana also had some terrible memories. One such memory is when Maybelle's mom and I got into a very heated argument over the phone. Dora is a loving and caring person, but she is extremely controlling and manipulative. She resembles me in many ways. It got to the point she was controlling our marriage and all our decisions. Dora and I had a very heated verbal argument and for several years the relationship was nonexistent. This was a very difficult time for Maybelle. She was torn between her mother and her husband. I became irrational. I prevented her mother from calling our home. I also prevented Maybelle from speaking to her mother when I was present. During the holidays, Maybelle would visit her parents and I mine, but never together.

We would spend little or no time together during our vacations to Miami. This went on for years. I know that I devastated Maybelle's heart with my behavior. I became obsessed with the hatred toward Dora. My hatred toward Dora was causing the greatest pain to Maybelle. My intentions were to protect Maybelle from her mother's controlling behavior not to cause more pain. I remember when Maybelle asked me whether her parents were allowed to come up for her graduation. I saw the tears in her eyes as I told her she needed to choose between her parents or me at graduation. In order for Maybelle not to upset her parents or me, she chose not to attend her own college graduation. She has always resented me for her absence during the graduation ceremony at Indiana University.

This is when my internal rage started. This is when the disease process began. It began slowly and subconsciously, but I know it started during this period of my marriage. My own pain and anguish were being projected onto those I loved the most. With every hateful and hurtful action demonstrated to those I loved, I would sink deeper into the waters of despair.

In my second year of graduate school, I became the victim of discrimination. Interestingly enough, it had nothing to do with sexuality, but with my Hispanic ethnicity. Indiana is notoriously a conservative state. Surprisingly enough, some of the local newspapers would announce the Ku Klux Klan town rallies. Actually, the Grand Wizard of the KKK lived only miles away in a neighboring town. It was a very disturbing and uncomfortable feeling hiding our ethnic heritage. We would take careful steps not to speak Spanish in public and avoid towns that were known to be racist.

It was 1988. I never imagined that I would be the victim of discrimination. I was the only Hispanic and there was only a handful of African-Americans in the program. Unfortunately, none of us stayed to finish our graduate program and I was forced to transfer to another university. Dr. Eales made my life a living nightmare. It was difficult to understand how such an educated man would make such derogatory remarks concerning minorities during his lectures. I can remember a lecture on Ocular Syphilis where Dr. Eales commented to the class that during our clinic rotations we would encounter patients with Ocular Syphilis. He continued to comment that the disease was not common except in lower economic populations. "For example", he said, "we will never examine Bill or Mary and diagnose Ocular Syphilis, but Jose and Jerome will most likely be infected with the spirochete." There were three minorities in the class. We all looked at each other in complete astonishment while the class giggled and laughed at Dr. Eales comments. Luckily, the courses were being audio taped and a collection of several of his remarks were documented. Afraid that reporting the incidents might affect my academic path, I said nothing to the school administration. Despite the many comments Dr. Eales made about minorities, I remained quiet. I continued to attend his lectures and strive to successfully complete my second year at Indiana University. One afternoon, I decided to visit his office for clarification on a confusing lecture topic. After much explanation and illustrations on the subject matter, I still wasn't grasping the concept. I noticed his frustration and then he angrily said, "You just don't have the mental capability to understand this topic." He went on to say, "It has been my observation that traditionally Blacks and Hispanics don't have the mental capability to understand abstract concepts such as these." I thanked him for his time and walked out of his small office speechless. I realized my second year was going to be tougher than expected. It was not until he failed me on my oral examination that I decided to pursue the allegations of discrimination against Indiana University. I hired an attorney and spoke to various human rights offices and began the biggest discrimination case against the university. The emotional roller coaster continued for several months. I had meetings with top academic officials, attorneys and many other individuals associated with the university. The stress was overwhelming and I requested to take the academic year as sabbatical. The dean of the university authorized my year sabbatical shortly after my request. This allowed me more time to pursue my legal case against the university. While on sabbatical, I worked as a substitute teacher for the town of Bedford, Indiana.

During my year sabbatical, I began to apply at various graduate programs throughout the United States. It was very difficult to convince the deans of other graduate programs to accept me considering I had a lawsuit against Indiana University. However, Nova Southeastern University granted me a transfer to their program. By this time, Maybelle had earned her Bachelor's in Social Work and we decided to move back to South Florida where the University was situated. We arrived in Hollywood, Florida where we rented an apartment near the school campus. We relocated a few miles north of Miami in a city called Hollywood. The apartment we rented was small, but had a large utility room that was used for our desks and bookshelves. Maybelle was accepted into Florida International University to begin her Master's program and I shortly was starting Nova Southeastern University. I began school in August 1990 as a second year student. The year went by relatively easy considering that there were many similarities in the courses between IU and NSU. It was difficult to come home and study because Maybelle was not at school at the time. Her program began in January 1991.

It just so happened that Maybelle and I saw Gary one day at the local shopping mall. We stopped and again exchanged phone numbers. Gary was accepted at the University of South Florida Medical School. After his first year at USF, he was put on academic probation. In his second year, Gary was expelled from USF. He applied to University of Miami Medical School and was accepted as a transfer student. Meeting Gary in the mall was not the best thing that happened to our marriage.

Gary was lonely and needed someone. Maybelle was needy and lacked companionship. Gary and Maybelle spent lots of time together fulfilling each other's needs. They would bar hop, go to the beach and visit the local mall where they shopped for hours. Meanwhile, I stayed home and studied. Several weeks into their close relationship, I began to be suspicious of an affair. However, I trusted Maybelle and knew she loved me. I would have never guessed she would have betrayed me.

By this time Maybelle and I were married six years. It was the summer of 1991. Our communication with each other was non-existent and our intimacy in and out of bed was nothing to brag about. I remember that just about the sixth year of marriage I stopped kissing Maybelle. I just stopped. I didn't know why, but the kissing simply seized. We would have mechanical sex. No passion nor foreplay, but just fucking. It was merely a mechanical action for both of us to *cum* and relieve our sexual needs. Our relationship was in trouble and I knew that nothing was wrong with her. I was the one with the problem. Something was happening inside me that I had no idea what it was. Gary knew our marriage was in trouble and he recognized Maybelle's vulnerability.

The friendship that Maybelle and I had developed began to disappear rapidly. With the loss of the friendship, we lost communication, then intimacy and finally sex. We would go for weeks without having sex. I was always reminded how many weeks it had been since our last sexual encounter. While having sex, Maybelle would ask me to kiss her. I never did. She would tell me how much she needed to be kissed, caressed and touched, but I simply would perform my mechanical husband duties and not acknowledge her needs. Don't misunderstand me, I wanted to make love to Maybelle, but I simply couldn't. Something inside of me was preventing me from behaving how a loving and caring husband should behave. It was heartbreaking to see her face as she asked for a kiss and I simply would tell her, "NO." It was painful for me to see her slip through my fingers not knowing what to do. I couldn't understand what was the matter with me. I would spend hours examining my emotional abusive behavior toward Maybelle only to end up with no solutions to our problems. I would spend hours trying to prepare myself mentally to kiss my wife, but I never did. I did everything to avoid sex. I would never go to bed at the same time with her. I would sleep fully dressed and if I woke up with an erection, I quickly took care of the situation secretly in the bathroom. Our marriage was going downhill quickly and we had no way to steer our relationship in the right path.

It was ironic that while Maybelle slept, I would caress her skin, touch her lips and speak softly in her ear. I would tell her everything she wanted to hear. I would caress her body how she wanted to be touched. I would apologize for my actions and swear that I would change. It was safe. I knew Maybelle would not respond back. It was safe for me to express the love I had for her while she slept. I felt that if I admitted my wrong doings to her she would ask me questions as to why I was behaving in such a monstrous fashion towards her. I hated questions. Questions meant that I needed to deliver explanations. I had no explanations why I emotionally abused her and despised her for no apparent reason. I was afraid that too many questions would open doors and allow my phantoms and secrets to seep out. I couldn't explain my feelings, thoughts and yearnings. Not then.

During these times of anguish and despair, Maybelle and I were putting on a show. We continued to pretend to be happy and continued our normal routine. Maybelle also continued her extracurricular activities with Gary. One evening, Maybelle, Gary, a mutual girl friend and myself decided to have some fun. We went out for a movie and pizza. On the way home, we decided to stop at a nearby convenience store. Gary and I left the girls inside the car and purchased several bottles of cheap wine. Actually, we bought seven bottles of *MD 20/20*. By the time we returned to our apartment, three bottles of the *medicine* was going through our bodies. We were in a state of intoxication, but determined to get more wasted as time continued. All four of us sat around the living-room table as the alcohol in our bodies did the talking. The conversations ran the gamut from A to Z. After several rather boring conversations, Gary motioned to play an adult version of Truth-or-Dare.

I wasn't born yesterday. I stopped my alcoholic consumption and tried to sober myself for the game. I needed to be alert and sober while I observed the dynamics of Maybelle and Gary. Specifically, I wanted to observe their interactions. I set some basic rules for the group game. One rule I stated was, "No sex with other partners." Everybody moaned in disappointed, but drunkenly agreed to the rule. The game started with simple truth questions, then it moved to more intimate questions. As the game continued, the game turned to dare. Soon after, we were daring each other to show our chests, our bare asses and even our dicks. I excused myself from the game to take a piss. I went into the bathroom and took a considerably long piss. When I returned, Maybelle and Gary's lips were locked in a tight seal. I simply and casually separated their bodies without saying a word. The game continued. Within several minutes, Gary was getting a blowjob from the other girl and Maybelle was doing the same to me. The room was dark and it was difficult to see Gary and Lina. I remember being sexually turned-on by the moans and groans coming from Gary as he was fucking Lina. With every moan, my own dick got harder and with every groan, my manhood came closer to exploding. I needed to see. I returned to the bathroom and turned the light on. I closed the door to the bathroom halfway allowing a gleaming ray of light to illuminate the sexual scene in the living room. As my eyes got acclimated to the light, I was able to see every motion and thrust that Gary was producing. My own dick was getting stiffer and closer to explosion as I observed Gary's naked body pounding Lina's. My eyes were fixed on him. All four of us were squirming throughout the floor in ecstasy. At one point, Gary's hairy ass fell on my left foot. I felt the crack of his hairy ass brushing up against my toe. I began to wiggle my toe very slightly in the same rhythmic motion as he. I didn't want him to move his body from my foot. I wanted to feel his hairy ass as long as I could; however, the intensity was to much for me to hold and I exploded my juice into Maybelle's mouth. Gary continued to fuck Lina awhile longer. After the exhausting sexual marathon was over, we all laid on the carpeted floor and fell asleep. Several hours into the evening, I woke and guided Maybelle into our bedroom.

In the morning, I was the first to awaken and the first to notice Gary's naked body lying on the carpeted floor. I quietly stepped into the kitchen where I secretly admired the beauty of his nakedness. He was face up and his dick was flaccid. I could easily see from my strategic observation point his bush as it continued down his balls and into the crack of his ass. I stayed for several minutes until my own dick started to get hard. I reached inside my boxers and started slowly stroking my hard cock. It was too risky, so I decided to finish the job in the bathroom. I knelt over the toilet where several squirts of white *cum* shot into the stagnant water. Several minutes afterwards, I returned to the kitchen only to witness that Gary was awakening from his sleep. He reached for his wrinkled shirt and stood up to sleeve his arms through it. The next to awaken was Maybelle and then finally Lina. No one mentioned anything about our previous night's adventure. It was as if nothing ever happened. Maybelle, Lina and Gary regarded the evening as a game; however, it was much more than a game to me. I became aware that the evening's sexual adventure was a catalyst for my secrets to surface again.

I began to work diligently suppressing my secrets. Of course, this meant becoming more distant with Maybelle. My internal frustration was increasing as hers with me. Gary knew there were problems in our castle. He saw the opportunity and began to throw some bait. Maybelle didn't take long before she was fished out of the water. I suspected soon after it began. I began to follow them everywhere. One early evening, I followed them to a park and saw my wife holding his hand and kissing his lips. I felt impotent. I thought to myself, *How could I blame her? I led her to cheat. I led her to be unfaithful. I led her to be kissed by another man. If only I would have or could have kissed her, she would not be in his arms.* My heart was torn into a thousand pieces. I remained in my car for two hours. After they left the park, I stayed in my car staring at the park bench where they sat and kissed. Tears rolled down my cheeks while realizing I was the culprit in my wife's betrayal.

The little I had remaining with Maybelle I threw it away. After seeing them at the park, I had no hope in reestablishing our love again. I separated myself emotionally and physically from her. I was falling deeper into an ocean of guilt. I had guilt about my buried secret and guilt that I led my wife to have an affair. The desperation was too intense for me to endure. I was literally drowning in my own sorrow and pain. Several months passed and Maybelle and I had not had sex. Everyday that passed became harder to get close to her again. Gary was no longer involved with our lives. He had moved to Ohio for his residency. Maybelle didn't know I was fully aware of her secret encounters with Gary and continued her life as before. As the weeks passed, I was becoming more emotionally distance from Maybelle. Finally, Maybelle couldn't deal with the rejection any longer and asked me what was the matter. I can still recall that evening.

I was in the spare bedroom working on the computer. The door was closed, but not locked. I heard a soft knock and the door softly opened to reveal Maybelle's worried face. She sat behind me on a small sleeper sofa. For several minutes, nothing was said. Then, Maybelle took a long sigh and asked me a question. "Do you know how many months it has been that we don't make love?" she asked. Again, I didn't reply. "I have been fantasizing about other men." she commented. At that point, I turned to her with disgust and asked her if she had reached orgasm with her fantasy men. She then pleaded with me to talk to her. I reluctantly agreed.

I began the rapport with the question, "Is there anything that you have not told me about?" "NO," she replied. The anger in my voice was now evident. I again asked her the same question and again she said, "NO." Fortunately, I kept a daily journal of Maybelle and Gary's affair. I reached for the small notepad with scribbled dates and short handwritten notes and handed it to Maybelle. I told her to read the contents and then we would have something to speak about. I turned back toward the computer and continued to work diligently. In the background, I heard her sobbing, but acknowledged nothing. Minutes later, she stood and came to hug me where I politely pushed her away.

I told her that the lack of sexual intimacy was due to the pain I was suffering knowing of her infidelity. I expressed why I couldn't touch her, kiss her or be intimate with her knowing that she had betrayed our love. I continued the attack. I made myself look good while she was ripped apart inside and out. The plan was to punish her and have me come out smelling like roses. As long as the affair was her fault, my own secret would continue to be buried and hidden. As long as she believed that my actions and rejection towards her were caused by her affair, I would be able to buy more time. The plan worked. I had managed to project my own guilt toward Maybelle. Soon afterwards, Maybelle felt that all the problems within our marriage were her fault.

I was relieved transferring my guilt to her. I wouldn't feel guilty any longer. I didn't have guilt when I yelled at her, when I didn't touch her or refused to kiss her. For the first time, I began to feel guiltless. I even felt inculpable when I fantasized about men and masturbated with my finger inside my asshole. I began to feel no remorse for my actions. I was changing. I was becoming a guiltless monster. A monster that was chiseled and sculptured by repressed anger, pain, despair, sorrow and sadness.

Chapter Five

Everyday we grew miles apart in our relationship and sexual intimacy. When we eventually made love, Gary's image would pop into my mind. I would mentally visualize him touching her, kissing her and making her feel, as I would never make her feel. I began to hate making love to my wife. Of course, I was only blaming her extramarital affair on my own sexual issues. It had nothing to do with Gary or the infidelity, but with what was happening to me. I began to fantasize more frequently with men while making love to Maybelle. It was horrible to have these images inside of me. When I would finally *cum*, a sense of relief would takeover my body. I felt proud. I felt that I was still a man capable of fucking my wife regardless of my sexuality.

My mind was becoming overwhelmed with thoughts of men. I remember the fantasies would first be sporadic. I would fantasize every several months about men and several weeks would pass before my next homoerotic fantasy. The gaps between the fantasies would be a respite allowing me to take control of my life. However, the gaps became shorter and shorter and the fantasies were lasting longer. I soon realized that the homoerotic fantasies were arriving monthly then weekly. It wasn't long before I was having male homoerotic fantasies daily. Everyday I would have to fight the demons that possessed me. Eventually, I would give in to the demonic demands. I would jerk-off everyday. Imaging myself with a man, I would masturbate in the bathroom late at night while Maybelle slept silently.

I would retrieve to the bathroom and lay on the floor naked. I would spread my legs and place them over the bathtub. I then greased my ass with plenty of hand lotion and reached for my insertion device. I would carefully and slowly penetrate my hole with Maybelle's hairbrush handle.

Slowly, it would enter my rectum giving me intense painful pleasure. With the brush handle halfway inside me, I would begin to thrust my ass against the tub inserting the pleasure device deeper and deeper inside. Thrusting my ass against the bathtub allowed my hands free to manipulate my cock. My dick was hard as a rock. I would put both hands around my 81/2-inch cock and begin to massage the throbbing rod until several long squirts of man juice came out from the piss hole. Slowly, I removed the hairbrush handle from inside my rectum leaving it sore and the rim swollen. I quickly cleaned the floor and wiped myself from the hand cream before returning to bed.

I needed to maintain a mental calendar of my jerking off sessions. I wanted to secretly masturbate everyday, but I needed to fuck my wife as well. Hence, I would reluctantly avoid self-gratification building up enough libido to have sex with her. The days when I did not masturbate, my rage and anger towards Maybelle was overwhelming. I would snap at her for no apparent reason. I would treat her unkindly and emotionally abusive. However, I was kind and sweet once I relieved myself in my private secret room. My behavior was sickening. I couldn't or didn't want to understand my behavior. All I knew was that I was a monster one day and a perfect husband the next. Of course, Maybelle was as confused as I was.

I was becoming an addict to male fantasies. For several years, my secret self-gratification sessions were all I needed to fulfill my sexual pleasures. But then, I became more daring. I would rent transsexual porno movies. I would watch them with Maybelle. The *she-males* would sexually excite me especially when another guy would suck their dicks. It became a habit to put on a video before Maybelle and I had sex. I would be able to function like a stallion while watching these smut films. Soon, the excitement of the *she-males* wore off and I began to rent bisexual male movies. However, I was too embarrassed to share these movies with my wife. I would watch them privately while she showered. I would watch small clips of the film making me sufficiently horny to fuck Maybelle after her shower. As I heard the shower water turn off, I would quickly eject the tape and hide the tape inside my desk drawer. Then, I would wait for her in bed ready to relieve my needs. Eventually, the newness of the videos also wore off and I needed more. I needed a new form of eroticism.

While watching the previews of one of the bisexual movies, I read an advertisement for the subscription to a gay magazine. Several days later, I called the toll free number and ordered the one-year subscription using Maybelle's name as recipient. It took six weeks for the first issue to arrive. I remember picking up the yellow envelop from our mailbox. I wanted to open the envelope, but I didn't. I waited for Maybelle to arrive home and thumb through her mail as she normally did. As she approach the yellow envelop, I began to sweat and my heart was beating faster. She finally opened the envelope to reveal the first of twelve issues of *Male Pictorial.* She thumbed through the pages quickly, but said nothing. She put the magazine inside the envelope and then made a comment. "What is this, a joke? I never ordered this," She said. I pretended not to listen as I continued to stare at the television set. She handed me the yellow envelope and then said, "Someone sent me this bullshit. Can you believe this?" I glanced at the glossy pages and simply giggled. Then, continued to watch my television program. She soon forgot about the monthly magazine arrivals, which allowed me to have sole possessions of the periodicals. Secretly, I kept them hidden away inside my desk.

I would go to my desk late at night and masturbate to the many pages of naked men. I would lock the door to my den and sit behind my desk. I would begin to take out the magazines and open the pages to my favorite pictorials. I would spread four or five magazines across my desk and lift my legs on the pickled oak desk. My ass would hang slightly off the chair giving myself easy access to my asshole. I then placed the small waste paper basket underneath the desk to collect my semen. My legs spread wide and my cock hard, I would begin to finger my hole with my left hand and masturbate with my right palm. Moments later, the white stream would squirt into the waste container.

I now had several avenues to relieve myself. The bathroom, the videos and my desk were all paradises for my sickness. My sickness became greater and greater and the fever was becoming more intense. Again, I had become disinterested in my new avenue of self-gratification. The bathroom sessions, the bisexual videos and the magazine subscription to *Male Pictorial* were not doing anything for me. I needed more.

In one of the magazines, I discovered an advertisement for phone sex. It took me several weeks to actually call the sex line. At first, I would hangup the receiver when connected to the other party. Eventually one evening at my desk, I dialed the number and decided to stay on line. "Hello, New York here," the deep voice on the other end said. "Hello," I replied. Then, the man began with a series of questions, "You hairy or smooth, top or bottom, cut or uncut? How big are you?" I answered the questions and realized that I had just told the strange voice that I was a smooth, cut, bottom and *5'11" tall*. He giggled and said, "Not how tall, but how big is your cock?" He then voluntarily gave me his stats, "39, hairy chest, stomach, arms and legs, 9 inches uncut and a total top." He then added, "You want to call me?" "Sure," I replied. He gave me his telephone number and I called him back within several seconds. He had a deep masculine voice. It was a seductive voice that caused my dick to get hard. He began to talk and instructed me what he was going to do to me. I couldn't say much except acknowledge his commands with mild moans of ecstasy. As he was penetrating me, I began to moan louder and louder. The pounding continued when finally I heard a long and powerful moan. "I'm *cumming*, I'm *cumming*," he said. "Ah, ah, ah, I'm *cumming*," he groaned. I too was shooting my load. I then hung up. I lay there with my legs on the top of my desk and dripping *cum*. I was astonished at what I had done.

The calls were directly charged to my telephone bill as "Adult Telecommunication Network". I didn't realize the cost of my new addiction until reality came in the form of the monthly telephone bill. The first month I had to pay over $ 500.00 in non-regulated phone calls. The expensive addiction was not a deterrent. I began to call the phone sex line often and soon became an addict to phone sex. My body would quiver with excitement as I would here the strange voice on the other end of the receiver shoot his load. Sometimes, I would enjoy a man so much that I would call him nightly avoiding the costly charges from the phone sex line company. I was creating more secrets to my already secretive lifestyle. I would worry if Maybelle entered my den, opened a desk drawer or pried into the telephone bill. Nonetheless, the addiction continued and the monthly charges rose higher and higher.

During one of my business trips away from home, Maybelle received a call from the phone company where it was brought to her attention that the phone service had not been paid. Maybelle expressed her concern to the phone company's agent and apologized for the delay in payment. She went to my den and began to search for the unopened bills. She came across the telephone statement and began to open the envelope. The charges were $382.00. Thank goodness she called me to explain her discovery before calling the phone company. She asked me about the non-regulated phone charges and I simply told her that the previous month the phone company had erroneously charged us a substantial amount as well. "There must be some kind of mix up with the computers," I reassured her. "I will be home in the morning. I'll call the phone company myself," I told her. She always hated to deal with the household finances and followed my advice diligently. I arrived the next morning and quickly made the check for the full amount owed to the telephone company. I drove to the nearby post office where I dropped the white envelope inside the blue mailbox. Several days later, Maybelle asked me if I had taken care of the phone discrepancy. "Yes," I told her. Nothing else was ever mentioned again.

Chapter Six

We were married eight years and our lives resembled the American dream on the outside. I finally became a doctor and Maybelle a mental health therapist. We were two young professionals striving to succeed. We moved from the apartment in Hollywood and purchased a small two-bedroom house in Tamarac. Tamarac is a small city about forty miles north of Miami. The neighborhood was a quiet and well-settled community. Our neighbors were older, Jewish and retired. Actually, we were the only young and Hispanic couple in the entire community. The community was notoriously known for disliking *breeders* because of their noisy children. However, Maybelle and I had no plans in the near future to have children. It was a small gingerbread house. The house was small, but adorable. It had a brick facade with emerald green window shutters. The porch had an emerald green flower box with lots of blooming perennials and the yard was carefully manicured to perfection. The shrubs nicely pruned and the landscape surrounding the house impeccable. The inside was comfortable, but tiny. The appliances were an avocado green color and the floor still had the original self-adhesive linoleum tiles. It was an old house, but very well preserved. Only one owner had lived in the tiny house prior to our purchase. She died one month previous to the purchase of our new homestead. The elderly lady's estate was left to a niece from New York. Fortunately for us, the niece was not interested in her aunt's furniture and we inherited several interesting antique pieces. Presently, several of the furnishings are in my possession and the remaining antiques are with Maybelle. In several months, we made this house into a beautiful chalet. We hung up pictures and wallpaper and bought several other pieces of furniture. Before we knew it, the small house was the nicest in the neighborhood. I loved our home.

Despite the charm we gave the house, we knew it was a starter home. Eventually, we would have to search for a more spacious home. As our financial resources grew, we began our search for a larger and more spacious house. Several months of investigation led us to a community fifteen miles south of Tamarac called Pembroke Pines. We purchased an empty lot and began construction of our future home. When complete, it would be a beautiful five bedroom home nestled in a suburb of Fort Lauderdale called Chapel Trail at the Pines. The house was very costly and we needed to save as much money as possible for it's construction. Therefore, we decided to rent our home in Tamarac and move into Maybelle's parents' house while our new home was under construction. By this time, my relationship with Dora was once again civil. For Maybelle's sake, we had managed to put our differences aside. We stuffed her parents' garage and two of their bedrooms with all our belongings. We paid no rent and ate their food everyday. It was a very profitable deal for us. We were saving so much money that we probably could have purchased a castle in Switzerland. However, we were modest and settled for a five bedroom house instead. We had it all. It was truly the American dream. Thirteen months after moving in with Maybelle's parents we moved into our new home. The same day we purchased a new car.

It was time to trade-in our blue Toyota Tercel. It was difficult to let go of this car, but the time came when it had to be done. The vehicle was more then ten years old and the air conditioner had not worked for several months. The engine would roar as if it was a diesel truck and the floor was rusted with a hole the size of a basketball. If you drove through a puddle, it was certain that your feet would get soaked. When it was raining, the sunroof would leak on your head. Despite the roars, holes and leaks, it was dependable. However, it was embarrassing driving the vehicle. We drove the blue relic into the Mercedes Benz dealership and several hours later, Maybelle was driving off the car lot with a white Mercedes Benz. I sat in the passenger seat and handed the car keys to her. I can still remember how beautiful and elegant she looked sitting behind the steering wheel of her new vehicle. I felt proud and accomplished. *We finally made it,* I thought to myself, as we drove off the lot leaving the blue Toyota Tercel behind.

We moved into our new house in 1993. The new home was gorgeous. We began to nestle ourselves inside and began to decorate every corner of every room. We had plenty of wall space and plenty of spare rooms. Within months, we managed to create another beautiful chalet. We began to add French doors to the master bedroom, high hat lighting throughout the house, brick *pavers* on the driveway and a swimming pool and hot spa in the back yard. Everything was done with exquisite taste and fashion. Unlike our previous neighborhood, Chapel Trail at the Pines was a younger and professionally upscale community. It was certainly a *breeders* neighborhood. Much to my dismay, I spent less than two years in that home. This house still holds some of the best memories I can recall as well as some of the worst.

During this time, Maybelle was director of a nursing home and I was a junior associate at an office in South Beach. South Beach is a predominantly gay neighborhood located in Miami Beach. It is a difficult city to work when you're a married gay man because of the temptations. It was an old office, but had much potential. I made a business deal with the owner that for the first year I would be a non-equitable partner with the provisions that the following year I would purchase fifty-one percent of the business. I would purchase an additional twenty-five percent of the business the following year and finally be sole owner the fourth year. The first several weeks were busy. I would arrive early morning and leave late in the evenings. I would have lunch at my desk and many times have dinner delivered to the office. It was a difficult time for me considering I was the *new kid on the block*. I had to familiarize myself with everything from the financial aspect to the medical portion of my new business. After several months of settling into my new position, I was able to arrive later to the office, leave at a reasonable time and enjoy an occasional lunch hour outside the office.

I would grab a deli sandwich and eat it while strolling down Lincoln Road Mall. Lincoln Road is a long strip of chic shops and boutiques, bookstores, antique stores and art galleries. Most stores are predominantly gay owned and operated. I would leisurely walk down the several blocks of shops sponging in the *gayness* of the atmosphere. My feelings were of astonishment and freedom as I walked the long strip of shops and stores. I would love to walk and *cruise* and be *cruised*. I would love to play the role of a gay professional and then quickly run away and hide into the safety of my straight life. I would sit on bus benches looking at the world that I was not a part.

Because of the demographics, I soon built a strong gay patient base. My business partner was older and well established and seemed to feel more comfortable with the geriatric population. It did not take long before our office was becoming very lucrative. Despite the office's lucrative financial rewards, my partner's personality was very difficult to handle. He was very set in his ways and disliked losing control of his office to a younger associate. Weeks before I was going to sign the contract deal to purchase fifty-one percent of the office, I realized that our business marriage needed a separation. I wrote my letter of resignation and left the office in good terms.

I was headhunted by a very prominent surgeon in Miami. He offered me a position to be a staff physician for a satellite office he was currently opening. I accepted the offer and opened the ophthalmology department in a new clinic in West Miami. It was challenging and tiresome, but I was earning a great salary and enjoyed what I was doing. Furthermore, it took me away from the boys in South Beach. Needless to say, I was not sexually active with men while working in South Beach. However, I new it was a matter of time before I tasted man-sex.

The new medical office resembled a factory. It was totally different than what I was used to in a private office. In my private office, I would see ten to twelve patients per day. This allowed me ample time to spend with my patients and establish the traditional patient/doctor rapport. In the new office, I was scheduled to examine forty-two patients daily. It was extremely frustrating and tiresome, but challenging. I was examining patients with a myriad of ocular diseases and soon realized how much I had forgotten since school and how much studying I needed to do. I would finish at the office late and drive home for dinner. After dinner with Maybelle, I would begin to read journal articles and textbooks for several hours. I was trying to keep current on all the latest ocular treatments for my new and exciting job. Or, I was simply trying to avoid any form of interaction with Maybelle. Within several weeks, I began to feel more comfortable and relaxed in my new office and soon was able to take my long overdue lunch hour that I enjoyed so very much. This is when the trouble started.

During my hour lunch, I would walk the corridors of a nearby shopping mall. I would have lunch at the courtyard and then relax myself window-shopping. I would do this routinely everyday giving myself a needed respite and relaxation from the assembly line of patients at the office. However, what I didn't realize was that a greater power was driving me closer to the depth of *queerness*.

I recall one afternoon while on my lunch hour that I needed to use the public rest room. While standing at the porcelain urinal, I got the uncanny feeling someone was watching me urinate. I quickly zipped my pants and left the rest room without even washing my hands. I was terrified at the notion that someone was looking at my dick while I took a piss. However, I felt more terrified at my erection than at the actual incident itself. Despite my fear, I returned the next day to the same rest room. I didn't have to piss, but I made myself stand at a porcelain urinal regardless. The bathroom was empty except for one man. He stood several feet away from me in front of the last urinal. I unzipped my dress pants and took out my limp dick. I stood there waiting for the urge to piss, but nothing came out. My ears were tuned to the sound piss makes as it hits white porcelain, but I heard only the absence of sound. I heard nothing. We just stood there. Quietly, we stood holding our piss empty dicks doing nothing. I began to see through the corner of my eyes that the man took a step back and he began to shake his cock. I questioned myself whether he was shaking off the last droplets of piss from his dick or was he stroking his cock? I wanted to look, but I couldn't. I tucked my dick inside my pants and again exited the rest room. It took me several daily visitations to the urinals before I felt comfortable enough to check out a man's dick. As I continued my daily routine visiting the busy rest room, my courage got stronger. The first several visits I would casually glance as strange men would fondle their hard dicks. It didn't take me very long before I was giving blowjobs to strange men in the mall bathroom. It didn't matter who they were. As long as they had a dick, I would fondle, stroke and suck their hard cocks. The adrenaline *rush* going through my body was exhilarating. I was sexually excited and at the same time fearful that I would be caught and arrested. The sensation of their penis in my mouth was incredible. I sucked dick every day and as much as I could. I would never get enough. I arrived at the mall by 12:05 and not leave the bathroom until 1:30 PM. I went from novice to amateur to professional dick sucker within a very short time period. The fear of getting caught and arrested was overwhelming. I was terrified. If ever I was arrested for such lewd behavior, I would not be able to work as a physician again. I thought of the embarrassment I would cause my wife and family as they found out the truth about me through the news of my arrest.

The fear of getting caught was too mentally exhausting. I slowly began to diminish my visits to the mall bathrooms and within several weeks I managed to decrease my bathroom sexual activities to once a week. I would entertain myself in other activities such as walking toward a nearby lake or having lunch with colleagues during my lunch hour. Despite my attempts to avoid the *cruising*, I discovered that wherever I went men *cruised* me. I felt that every gay man was able to tell I sucked dick. I would be *cruised* everywhere. Or maybe, it was the other way around, I would *cruise* everyone.

When I didn't suck dick for several days, I would begin to feel trapped and caged in my own body. I felt the need to have a dick in my mouth all the time. The temptations to suck dick were too powerful to control and once again, I fell victim to the sickening and disgusting bathroom sex scene. I began to avoid my colleagues for lunch allowing me time to visit my secret sex places.

Through my extensive search for secret rendezvous places, I discovered another nearby shopping mall where the bathrooms were less risky and the toilet stalls were completely private. The toilet stalls were concrete brick walls from floor to ceiling. The stall doors came down to the floor preventing anyone looking underneath the door. Each toilet stall was totally enclosed preventing unwanted observers looking inside. On my second visit to my new treasure hunt, I was invited to enter a stall. The stalls were small with enough space for one individual. However, in this stall, there were two other guys anxious to suck dick. I lowered my pants giving them access to my hard cock. While one guy was sucking my dick, the other man was hungrily eating my ass. Ferociously, they ate at their man-meal at both ends until I was moaning from the excruciating pleasure. I was thrusting my dick further inside his throat when I reached orgasm. My white thick load dribbled down the sides of his mouth like white foam from a rabied dog. I became a frequent visitor to the men's room and soon I was able to recognize familiar faces. I recall an afternoon when two colleagues and I went to the shopping mall for lunch. As we were walking toward the food court, a man said "hello" to me. I was mortified at the notion that my colleagues were going to figure out that the strange man was gay or worse, that I was.

It wasn't long before I began to do more than suck dick. The privacy of these stalls gave me the privilege to rim some hairy asses. It wasn't easy to rim a man's ass inside a small cubicle, but with determination and imagination it was possible. It didn't happen very frequently, but the few times it did occur it was very much enjoyed. I would tell the man to squat at the edge of the toilet facing the water toilet tank. I would bend my knees and get in position. I would tongue their sweaty ass clean and at times finger their man hole as well. A few of these men wanted me to fuck them, but I never did.

My addiction to anonymous sex became stronger and stronger. I was spending more time at public bathrooms and *cruisy* places than at the office. I developed a keen sense of knowledge where the best *cruising* places were located. I would visit these places and *cruise* them for potential sex. I made notes in my memo pad recording the best locations and best times to visit these sex chambers. It was a rather tedious task to scribble such information, but it saved me lots of time visiting places that were not action packed on certain times and days of the week.

Through my extensive homework, I managed to discover a very *cruisy* location. It was the Florida Turnpike service plaza rest rooms. Here, I would spend endless hours in the morning before arriving at the office and endless hours after leaving the office prowling for sex. I would meet men in the rest rooms and then take them inside my car where we would masturbate or perform other "fun" stuff. Still, the fear of an arrest was present, but not enough to halt my addictive sexual behavior.

I recall one man I met in the service plaza rest room. He was no older than twenty-three and gorgeous. He was handsome, tall, dark, and hairy. As he stood next to me at the urinal, I glanced down to his crotch and observed a beautifully erect penis. He became aware of my stare and stood back allowing me to have a better view of his manhood. He was certainly well made. He invited me to his car and I agreed. It was broad daylight and several vehicles were around us. He didn't seem to care. He pulled my dick out and began to suck. He sucked on my shaft relentlessly. He continued to nurse my cock until I was screaming from the pleasure his warm mouth was giving me. I told him I was getting close to the point of explosion, but he didn't care. He wanted my stream of hot *cum* to enter his mouth. I shot my load into his mouth and felt him swallowing gulps of the white juice. He continued to stroke and suck my dick nursing the last drops of *cum* milk from my piss hole. After he sucked me dry, he reach over and began to tongue kiss me. I tasted my own *cum* and felt a new hard-on between my legs. It was his turn. I began to work him as he did me. I didn't have to work him much before he shot his load into my mouth. I tasted that man juice trickling down my throat and I was in ecstasy. We kissed and exchanged telephone numbers. I gave him a falsified telephone number and never called his.

I recall another instance when I was *cruising* a restroom in one of these service plazas and a man stood next to my urinal. He was blond and in his late thirties. He was wearing a dress shirt, tie and dress slacks. He was also very handsome and appeared to be nervous. I showed my dick hard and slightly leaned back from the urinal for him to look at my manhood. As I was checking him out, I noticed what appeared to be a pair of handcuffs protruding from the back of his waistband. Regardless whether the hidden item were handcuffs or not, I panicked. I quickly zipped myself up and headed outside the building. My knees were weak giving me trouble reaching my car. I sat inside my vehicle and momentarily lost conscious. It must have been seconds later when I woke up and saw myself draped over the steering wheel. Today, I realize it was the adrenaline *rush* that was streaming through my body that caused me to faint. I never found out whether the handsome man was a decoy police officer or not. This incident allowed me to evaluate my sexual promiscuousness. I decided to cut my prowling to a minimum. Despite my good intentions, it was only a matter of time when the sickness of my sexual addiction made me *cruise* again regularly.

Chapter Seven

Maybelle and I decided on a vacation. We decided on the Western Caribbean islands as our destination. We booked a cruise and made plans to sail from Miami to Mexico. It was a vacation that was long overdue. We were falling farther apart and felt that a vacation would rekindle our intimacy. It was a vacation she needed and definitely deserved. I remember on the way to the port of Miami Maybelle saying to me, "This vacation will be our second honeymoon." I simply acknowledged her statement and continued to drown in my own thoughts and sorrow. She planned for this trip with great enthusiasm and joy. It had been many years since we were able to take a vacation primarily due to my school schedule and our financial resources.

As we were entering the ship, the cruise personnel were on the main deck greeting their weeklong passengers. I knew I was in deep trouble when I caught the eyes of the cruise cinematographer. He was the most beautiful man I had ever seen. He was filming the passengers as they entered the ship to later sell the videotape as memoirs of our sea adventure. As he saw me, he casually put his large video camera down from his shoulder and stared. He locked his blue eyes on mine like a missile on an enemy target. He politely greeted us, but never looked at Maybelle. His name was Geoff.

He was slightly shorter than myself with short salt and pepper hair. He must have been in his early to mid thirties and had a beautiful masculine face. His body was perfect. He resembled a Greek athlete. It didn't take me long to discover Geoff's whereabouts and schedule. Early the next day, I went to the gym. I did my usual hour workout and proceeded to the locker room where I took a quick cold shower. After showering, I walked passed the steam room and sauna and decided to relieve my aching muscles by entering the sauna. The hot chamber was too enticing to pass up. I entered the sauna with my wet towel loosely wrapped around my waist. I sat down on a hot wooden bench and looked to my side. Diagonally from me, Geoff was lying on his back. He casually turned his head toward me and smiled. He had his towel loosely covering his crotch revealing the full extent of his massive legs and thighs. He removed the towel exposing his hard cock. It was thick and long resting on his stomach. I couldn't keep my eyes off his dick. My breathing was becoming more labored and the sweat beads were rolling down my entire body from the heat in the small sauna. I noticed that his dick had a thin white string of *precum* dripping on his stomach. As his dick throbbed, the *precum* oozed more. He would reach over with his index finger and touch the head of his dick interrupting the continual flow of *precum*. I also unwrapped my towel around my waist revealing my hard cock. He stood up from his supine position and moved closer to me. His hard dick still dripping with translucent juice as he continually massaged it. He put his hand around my cock and without warning lowered his head toward my crotch. He put my pulsating dick in his mouth and began to ferociously suck me. I kept pushing myself back preventing an early ejaculation. Finally, I reach over and held his dick in my hand. His dick was so hard it felt like an ore of steal inside my hand. I began to stroke his manhood for several minutes while he moaned and groaned in ecstasy. Within minutes, his dick was squirting white *cum* on the bench. I put the palm of my hand over his dick as the last drops of man juice squirted out. I used his last few drops of *cum* to lubricate my own strokes as I masturbated. He took his towel and gently wiped the dripping *cum* from my stomach. As he was doing so, he softly told me, "I'll be here in the mornings and around eight o'clock in the evenings." The cruise was seven days long and I never missed a date with Geoff.

Geoff and I began to establish more conversation during our brief meetings. I learned he was from a small town in Tennessee where he lived until he became a member of the ship crew. He told me his last name and revealed he was bisexual. He confessed he had a girlfriend who also worked on the ship and therefore he needed to be careful and discreet about his activities. I reassured his worries by telling him I was married and my wife was also on the ship. He reported to be happy in his relationship, but enjoyed the company of men. I knew better. He was as *queer* as me, but couldn't deal with the issue of homosexuality. Deep inside his soul, I was sure that he was not happy with his life.

Our sessions were becoming longer everyday. While keeping a careful eye, we would engage in more daring sexual activities. It was very nerve wrecking being the lookout while sticking my tongue in his ass. We wanted more privacy, but I couldn't bring him to my cabin nor I visit his. We needed to explore our bodies thoroughly and completely. I wanted desperately to make love to him and him to me. I desperately yearned to have him inside me. During one of our public demonstrations of affection, we noticed a tall, white handsome man enter the sauna. He didn't care to wrap a towel around his 6-inch hard cock as he entered the sauna. I supposed he knew we were *queer* before he even entered. His name was Steve. Geoff and I were sitting next to each other and Steve chose the bench directly opposite to us. He sat and immediately began to fondle his small member giving us permission to continue our deviant behavior. Geoff and I continued where we left off prior to Steve entering the hot chamber. We took turns sucking each other's dick and rimming our assholes while Steve watched and stroked his own dick. At one point, I straddled Geoff and held both our dicks in my right hand while simultaneously stroking both our members together. As I was doing so, I felt Steve's hand on my buttocks gently caressing my cheeks. Both hands kneading my ass cheeks as though they were bread dough. Steve's hand began to move toward the center and it wasn't long before I felt several fingers massaging the rim of my ass. I could feel my hole wet with sweat as he continued to push his fingers inward. Finally, one of Steve's fingers entered me and shortly after another digit went inside my asshole. He continued to move his two fingers in and out rhythmically while I stroked our dicks. Geoff and I managed to shoot our loads at the same time and moments later, I felt Steve's *cum* squirting on my buttocks. Steve suggested meeting the following day at his cabin. He mentioned that he was traveling alone and had a comfortable large bed in his cabin. I accepted his invitation without any reservation. Geoff was more reluctant, but agreed to meet at Steve's cabin the following morning.

I was the first to get to Steve's cabin. Moments later, I heard a knock at the door and Geoff entered the room. Geoff was the first to pull down his uniform pants and underwear exposing his perfectly erect cock. Steve took it upon himself to pull my shirt off and lower my shorts and underwear to my ankles. I lowered my head and began to suck Geoff's dick and Steve sucked on mine. It was three bodies intertwined into one. I remember my dick was so hard it was hurting. Geoff threw me on the bed and began to rim my ass. As he rimmed, Steve sucked me. We took turns giving each other pleasure. However, my focus was on Geoff. Finally, after a one-hour session we began to masturbate each other. Steve and I shot our loads on Geoff and then I stroked Geoff's cock until his load spilled out onto his hairy stomach. It was a pool of *cum* on his hairy belly. We cleaned each other and kissed good-bye. Geoff and I met the next day in the locker room chamber to exchange sexual pleasures again. Steve, Geoff and I met on two other occasions where we had several hours of more private and intimate sexual interludes. Needless to say, the cruise was awesome.

Unfortunately, Maybelle was not receiving the same sexual gratification as I. She continually reminded me of the lack of sexual interest I had toward her. Despite her many requests, I never fucked her during our trip. I remember one night she asked me why we hadn't had sexual intercourse and I simply told her that I was very tired from our busy itinerary. I saw the pain in her eyes as she processed my lame excuse. My guilt was so towering that in Cancun, Mexico I surprised her with an astonishing gift.

Maybelle and I went inside a diamond house to look at diamonds. Believe it or not, Mexico has very good quality stones. Most of their superior quality diamonds are mined from Russia and imported to Mexico. She didn't understand why we were looking at such precious stones, but I did. I wanted to buy her something expensive to take away my guilt. I asked the well-dressed Mexican diamond broker to show me several stones. I gave him a price range and he instructed us to follow him to the safe. We sat in front of a small black velvet-top table. On one side were Maybelle and I and on the other side the well-dressed diamond broker with two incredibly handsome bodyguards beside him. After several hours, I decided on three stones that were almost flawless. The three stones were each one-karat. One round cut diamond stone and two one karat each trillion cut diamonds. We then proceeded with choosing the mounting for the stones. Meanwhile, Maybelle couldn't believe her eyes. The Mexican man reached for his phone and called someone. Several minutes later, a younger man entered the heavily guarded room. He sat next to the diamond broker and told us that he would design the band for us. He asked Maybelle several questions and shortly began to sketch several bands on paper. After many sketches, he asked us to choose our four favorite illustrations. We did. He opened his lap top computer and the sketches were now becoming three-dimensional. Our decision was made quickly. We chose a broad gold band with the center one karat round cut diamond sitting high on a four-prong crown. On each side of the center stone and half embedded into the band of gold were the two one karat each trillion cut diamond stones. He measured her left hand ring finger and told us that the masterpiece would be finished the next day. I paid half of the total price as earnest money and we both left the gem house exhilarated.

Maybelle and I arrived the next day around eleven in the morning. The well-dressed Mexican gentleman remembered us immediately and showed us the way to the safe once again. He emptied the contents of a black velvet bag revealing the gold and diamond masterpiece. Maybelle's eyes opened with excitement as she saw the astonishing beauty of gold and diamonds. The gentleman gave me the ring and told me to try it on her. Maybelle stretched her shaking left hand and I placed the ring on her finger. I have never seen her eyes sparkle with such excitement. She hugged me and kissed my lips tenderly as she whispered, "Thank you." This made her happy for the rest of the trip and it made me feel guiltless about my promiscuity. The sex continued with Geoff in the mornings and evenings for the remainder of our voyage. However, I felt no guilt. I had bought my wife a $7,000.00 diamond ring.

We finally docked into the port of Miami after seven exhausting days. It took several hours to be cleared by customs and by mid morning we were outside waiting for a taxi to take us home. As we waited for a cab, Steve walked passed us. He looked at me then glanced at Maybelle standing beside me. I was afraid he would say something, but he didn't. I was terrified that he was going to expose our secret to Maybelle. However, he simply walked passed me with the grace of a true Englishman.

We arrived at my parents' home late morning and both my parents and Maybelle's parents were waiting for us. Maybelle showed off the expensive ring and I was still thinking about Geoff. I couldn't stop thinking about him. I became obsessed with him. All I thought about was our secret rendezvous together and our romantic walks on the moonlit decks while Maybelle slept in our cabin. I thought I was in love.

I decided to call the cruise line and ask how I could contact Geoff. I explained that I was a passenger and needed to write a short "Thank you" note for his hospitality. The cruise personnel were very helpful and soon gave me the address where I could write. I wrote several short letters to him, but received none from him. The last letter I wrote to him was to tell him that I would be waiting for him at the dock upon the ship's return from her next voyage. As promised, I was there waiting for him on Sunday morning. It took several hours of patiently waiting before I noticed the ship's crew parading through the side gates of the pier. I walked near the gate and stood waiting for Geoff. I felt like a wife waiting for her soldier returning home from war. About one hundred men and women walked passed me dressed in uniform and civilian clothing. I then noticed Geoff several hundred feet behind the green iron gates. He was wearing a white shirt and tight jeans. He was holding a backpack over his shoulder and next to him was a woman. They continued to walk toward the gate and my heart began to race. Finally, it was time. I had made plans to take him to a quiet lunch in South Beach and then I would hand him a key to the hotel room. I made reservations at a hotel in the beach where we would spend five hours together before he had to board the ship again. Geoff was three feet in front of me when I softly called his name. He turned to me and simply continued to walk ignoring my presence. I was heartbroken. I called his name a second time, but Geoff never turned around. Whatever his reasons for ignoring me, left me heartbroken. I put the puppy love behind me and continued on with my life. Nonetheless, the cruise was truly the turning point of my sexuality.

I arrived home later that afternoon in a melancholy state. I was truly heartbroken and very emotionally confused about my own feelings. The days passed and my sadness evolved into a mild depression. Maybelle would ask me what was the matter and I couldn't answer her. *How could I tell her about the feelings I had about Geoff? How could I tell her what happened during the seven day Caribbean vacation?* I couldn't. I had to keep my silence. The depression continued for several weeks until finally I needed to vent. I asked Maybelle to come inside the bedroom where I had spent most of the time sleeping since our arrival from our trip. I told her I needed to express my feelings to her and that I didn't want her to judge me in any way. Maybelle sat at the edge of the bed and gave me permission to begin speaking.

I expressed to her that I was indeed depressed. I told her about my feelings which I didn't seem to understand nor comprehend. "Feelings," I said, "about men and wanting to hold men." She said nothing. I continued to tell her how much I needed to embrace another man. She said nothing. I continued with my illusive comments for several minutes without any interruptions from Maybelle. After I finished, she simply held me in her arms and said, "I believe that what you are feeling is the love that you never had from your father. Maybe, you want to feel that love from a man because you have never felt that love from your own father." I should have been more honest with her, but how could I have told her the truth? How could I have told my wife that what I wanted was not simply to embrace a man, but to make love to a man? I wanted to tell her the truth, but I simply couldn't. She began to stroke my hair, which always relaxed me, and soon thereafter I fell asleep. The topic was never brought to light again. I self-prescribed *Prozac* and within several weeks I was less melancholy and able to function more normally. Several months followed when I realized that I had not had sexual intimacy with a man. It seemed that I had licked the homosexuality completely. Much to my amazement and unannounced, the urges for men returned to haunt me.

I applied for a position as an adjunct faculty instructor at a local university. I was hired several weeks later as a faculty member for the university teaching Anatomy and Physiology. I had always enjoyed teaching and despite the nominal wages I was enthused at my new job. During the day, I would work at my office and then commute thirty miles to the university campus to teach my two lectures. What I wasn't aware was the availability for sex with men throughout the university campus. I usually arrived early to prepare for my lectures. I would take my course materials to the library where I would prepare for class.

While sitting in the library on the fourth floor I decided to go to the rest room to piss. As I opened the men's bathroom door, I heard two stall doors quickly close. My intuition told me that there were two guys enjoying themselves sexually. I entered the last stall and noticed a glory hole on the stall wall. When I finished emptying my bladder, I glanced at my watch. I had about forty-five minutes to spare. I lowered my pants and sat on the toilet seat. It didn't take very long before my stall neighbor was tapping his foot. I knelt on the floor giving my stall neighbor access to my hard dick. He maneuvered his head through the bottom opening and began to suck my cock. I heard the last stall open and footsteps approaching my stall. I opened my door and saw a beautiful young student with his dick hard as a rock protruding from the zipper hole of his shorts. Without invitation, I began to give him a blowjob. It wasn't long before the other stranger opened his door demonstrating his manhood. We all took turns giving each other blowjobs. I shot my load first and quickly afterwards one of the students followed. I didn't stick around to watch the other student ejaculate. I rapidly washed my hands and returned to my table. I gathered my paperwork and left the library. I entered my lecture auditorium and stood at the podium waiting for the students to enter the room. I would look at every male student's face that entered the lecture hall hoping that no one resembled the two boys I had sucked moments before. None of the ninety-eight students had any resemblance and I was able to continue with my lecture. It had been months since my last sexual contact with another man, but it only took seconds for my addiction to come back. It wasn't long before I discovered the whereabouts of other *cruisy* places. I was visiting the rest rooms all throughout campus. I would jerk-off with other men between class breaks and after my lectures. It was sickening. Despite the fear of getting recognized by a student, I continued my sexual addiction.

One evening after my last lecture, I decided to visit a rest room. I stood at the last urinal awaiting my victim. The bathroom door opened and a young dark skinned student entered. He chose to stand two urinals away from me. I glanced at him and gave him a sense of ease and permission to look at my hard dick. As he looked down at my dick, I began to stroke my cock. I gestured for him to come closer and he obliged. As he bent over to suck me, I put my left hand inside his shorts rubbing my hand over his hairy butt. I forced my middle finger inside his hole and he began to moan and groan. I continued my *fingering* as he continued to suck me. With his right hand, he was stroking his *uncut* dick back and forth. He continued to relax his sphincter allowing deeper penetration. I heard his moans deeper and his breathing harder as his palm was wet with his own *cum*. I took possession of my dick and began to stroke. After the first squirt of semen, the student wrapped his hand around my cock and continued the stroking until he milked it dry. I left the rest room and began to walk towards my office in the Biology building. I opened the door to the suite of offices to check my mail slot. Minutes later, I turned off the lights and began to head toward the glass door. Just as I was about to open the glass door and step outside, the dark skinned student was walking down

the hallway. We looked at each other and then he stopped. He stood waiting for me as I continued my departure from the office. As I was locking
the office door, he came behind me and asked me if I was a teacher. I said,
"Yes." He then said, "*Cool.* Will I see you again?" "Yeah," I replied. I did
meet up with him on several occasions simply because I was concerned
about what he could do or say to the university officials. I was afraid of
him. As far as I know, he never said anything to anyone. It was his secret
and probably his fantasy to suck a professor's dick. I made his fantasy
come true. My sexual addiction continued to grow, bloom and worsen. I
was consumed with the obsession of having sex with men everywhere.

Even though the dark skinned student was harmless, the luck was soon
to end. I frequented a bathroom near my lecture hall that was also a busy
meeting place for sexual exchanges. The toilet stalls had a glory hole large
enough that my entire dick would go through to the other side. Before my
lecture, I would visit the rest room and enjoy a quick blowjob. Most of the
times, I wouldn't *cum*. I was just interested in the blowjob. The visitation
became a daily ritual. Fortunately, someone was always waiting for me on
the other side to give me pleasure with their warm mouth. I continued
this exercise on a daily basis for several weeks.

While grading the first exam papers, I came across one test paper that
was left blank. The individual didn't attempt to answer any of the questions. It was void of any ink markings except for his name and Social
Security number on the top margin of the paper. Of course, I gave him an
"F" as a grade. Below his grade, I wrote, "See me." As I was returning the
test papers, I called upon the name of the student that had earned the low-
est grade in the class and handed him the exam paper. He was blond and
relatively not an attractive young man. He must have been no older than
nineteen-years-old. I discussed the entire examination with the class clari-
fying any questions my students might have had. Then, I continued with
my lecture. At the end of the lecture, I asked the students to please return
all the exam papers. I never allowed students to keep my examinations.
When the lecture ended and everyone had left the classroom, the blond

student handed me his test paper. He scratched off the "F" and wrote an "A" instead. He stood in front of the podium expressionless. I thumbed through the pages and on the last page he wrote, "I have been sucking your dick for several weeks. I think I deserve a better grade." I rapidly took the paper and placed it inside my briefcase and quickly left the room. I did record an "A" in the grade book. Actually, the blond student earned "A's" on three subsequent exams and never attended class. I couldn't wait for that semester to end. I felt that I was going to be arrested by the campus police and the local newspaper was going to put my picture on the front page. The headlines would read, "*University Professor Arrested for having Sex with Male Students in Public Rest Rooms.*" Once the semester finally ended, I never took another teaching job again. Despite the scare, I continued to have sex with men. I chose the local shopping malls and interstate service plazas as my means to meet men.

I had finally learned to juggle my dual life quite easily. I was jerking off with men several times a week and allowing myself days to be intimate with Maybelle. Usually, my period of rest would be during the weekends. The weekends allowed me to build enough libido to fuck Maybelle on Saturdays or Sundays. Our lives seemed perfect. We had a beautiful home and successful careers. We couldn't ask for anything else from life. Well, Maybelle was asking for more. She needed a baby. In the past, I had made up several excuses why we should not start a family. There was the excuse of "We just got married," "We are too young," "We are both in school," "We just finished school," etc. However, I had no more excuses. It was time to have a family. We began to try and try and try without any success. We attempted for several months before realizing that there might be a medical problem. Maybelle took the initiative and made an appointment with a fertility doctor. After many examinations, the doctors discovered that Maybelle was barren and needed medical intervention to have children. I was relieved that the medical problem was not with me. Maybelle was put on very high dosages of medication promoting her ovaries to function normally. Such high dosages were carcinogenic and it was a very difficult decision to continue with the cycles month after month. Each therapy cycle was a three-month duration. I told Maybelle in December 1994 that this would be the last cycle she would be on due to the increase danger of ovarian cancer. She reluctantly agreed with me and we continued with the last therapy cycle. The doctors would instruct us on when we could have sex. I mean, they exactly told us what hour in the morning, afternoon or evening we would have sexual intercourse. The strict time frame had to do with Maybelle's ovulation. It became a job to have sex not a pleasure. But then again, it was never a pleasure. Finally, it wasn't long before the scheduled sexual tasks prevented my dick from responding properly. I just couldn't get a hard-on. The last month of the cycle was March 1995. Maybelle and I were scheduled for sexual intercourse the last two days in February and the first day in March. I couldn't. My dick couldn't get hard. She tried everything within her powers, but I just couldn't get my dick hard. Finally, she became upset and left the house. She arrived an hour later with three porno movies. There was one movie about bisexuals another video about transsexuals and the third porno flick was a straight video. She inserted *Bi and Beyond* into the VCR hoping for a miracle. No miracle occurred. She attempted the other two movies only to be left with more disappointment. She went to bed upset realizing that was her last cycle in our yearlong therapy. Several hours later, I decided to do something.

I went into the bathroom and grabbed a syringe and a small Dixie cup. I removed the needle from the plastic syringe and laid it on the bathroom countertop. While Maybelle slept, I began to masturbate as I often did. It wasn't long before the massaging of my prostate allowed my dick to get hard. Left hand finger in my hole and right hand wrapped around my dick, I began to stroke my cock. Just before shooting my load, I removed my fingers from my hole and got hold of the small paper cup. Placing the cup over the head of my dick, white cream oozed toward the bottom of the yellow flowered Dixie cup. I placed the sperm filled cup on the countertop while I wiped the hand cream from my asshole and washed my hands. I took the specimen to Maybelle and gently woke her. I told Maybelle that I was going to artificially inseminate her with my sperm. I opened Maybelle's legs as wide as I could then placed a pillow under her waist propping her vagina at an incline. I sucked up as much *cum* into the syringe and entered the long plastic tube carefully inside her pussy. I slowly continued to push the syringe inward until I felt the tip touch the cervical area. I began to push the contents of the syringe inside of her vagina. After squeezing the last sperm cell out of the *needleless* syringe, I raised her legs over her head allowing gravity to continue the migration process. Several days later she got her blood test. It was positive. Finally, after many months of giving her injections and spending countless hours at the doctor's office, Maybelle conceived (artificially) on March 1, 1995. Exactly nine months later, on December 1, 1995, God blessed us with a beautiful, healthy baby girl.

I remember her call. She was crying from the news as she said to me, "I'm pregnant! I'm pregnant!" I simply responded, "Congratulations! Our lives have changed." I realized on March 1, 1995 that my life was cemented into heterosexuality. I felt no joy in becoming a father, but rather desperation instead. I felt overwhelming guilt bringing a child into my world.

During Maybelle's pregnancy, I made a conscience effort to change my life. I wanted to be a good husband and father. I decided to stop the excessive *cruising* for man-sex in public places. I stopped the daily phone sex and halted my private jerk-off sessions in our bathroom. For the first trimester, I was an exemplary heterosexual husband. I was excited about my wife's pregnancy and my new role as a father-to-be. It seemed that I had licked my sexual desires completely. Then, my anger started again. This time it was more intense and severe. I would project my anger to Maybelle for no apparent reason. I would snap and lash at her with hurtful words not knowing why I was doing it. I began to hate Maybelle, my home, my career and my entire life. I tried to suppress my homosexual feelings, but the more I repressed my fantasies the more angry I got. I ultimately was becoming a caged monster. I realized that the need to act out my sexuality was essential and in her second trimester I began to *cruise* for man sex again.

I rationed myself to anonymous sex once or twice a week, but soon it was back to the usual five or six times per week. I visited the same places that months prior were in my daily agenda. My internal turmoil grew stronger and more powerful. I was sick to my stomach as I held my pregnant wife every night knowing what I had done with a man hours before. I began to feel worthless and soon afterwards another mild depression returned. Despite my depression, I continued to play around with men.

Maybelle was eight months pregnant when I met Mario. I was strolling in the mall when we noticed each other's stare. He walked passed me and our eyes locked. He was shorter than myself with dark hair and green eyes. His body was a chiseled masterpiece sculpture. His forearms had an even fur of hair from his knuckles to his biceps and through the top of his crew neck were several locks of dark hair visible. His face was masculine and clean cut. His gym shorts were tight around his thighs. His thighs were strong, muscular and with the same masculine fur that covered his entire body. I couldn't let him slip by me. I followed him through the mall until it was evident that I was *cruising* him. I followed him inside several stores and he did the same. We continued the cat and mouse game for several minutes. At one instant, he gently grabbed his crotch while staring into my eyes, which in gay sign language means: *I want you NOW.* I followed him to a nearby rest room where we stood next to each other in front of the urinals. Unfortunately, the rest room was full of several *queers* and I wasn't in the mood to share my prize. I whispered for him to follow me to another location.

We finally reached another rest room where it was empty. We both stood side-by-side in the urinals and unzipped our pants. My dick was difficult to take out due to the intense hard-on. His was a little more flaccid and easier to expose. However, once I exposed his manhood, his dick became as hard as mine. His cock was long and thin with a small sperm sac. He lowered his shorts below his knees and raised his shirt up to his nipples. He was aware of the beauty of his body and wasn't shy to show it off. Exposing his half naked hairy body was enough to cause my ejaculatory volcanic explosion. We both stood there stroking each other's dicks. I was stroking him with one hand and caressing the fur of hair on his butt with my other hand. His dick was a constant stream of *precum* as I continued to massage his body and cock. I lost track of time. I felt we were there for thirty minutes or longer. I lowered his shorts to his ankles and raised his shirt above his head. I continued to caress his body while I licked him all over. I felt lost in time. I was so sexually excited that my dick began to ejaculate without stroking. I reached for his dick and began to stroke. As he groaned and moaned louder demonstrating his "closeness", I turned Mario toward me and he shot his load on my bush. Once he shot his load, we gave each other a small peck on the lips and quickly got dressed. I was warm from the heat of excitement as I felt his *cum* drip from my bush to my balls and down my hairy ass. He wrote his name and telephone number on a small piece of paper and gave it to me. I drove home still feeling the wetness trickling down my hairy ass. I arrived home and quickly showered removing the dried crusty semen from my crotch and ass. I decided to go directly to bed after my long shower.

The next day I couldn't keep my mind off Mario. I couldn't concentrate on my drive to the office, my patients or anything at all except him. I kept his telephone number and name inside my wallet for several weeks. The obsession with Mario grew larger and larger and finally I decided to call him. Fortunately, he wasn't home and I was able to leave a message on his voice mail instructing him to call me at his convenience. On the way home from the office, my car phone began to ring. On the third ring, I answered and it was Mario. The conversation was awkward at first, but within several minutes I felt more comfortable speaking to him. Fifteen minutes into our conversation and only a few blocks from my home, he asked me out on a date. *A date with a man,* I thought, it sounded so foreign to me. I didn't have enough time to continue the conversation and told him I would call him in the near future.

I remember one day soon after my initial encounter with Mario arriving home late from the office and opening the door to my house when I noticed the house was dark. The house had an aroma of cooking spices and herbs. I went toward the kitchen and noticed a complete dinner being prepared. I looked around the entire house and saw no one. As I walked toward our bedroom, I noticed a shimmering light coming from the master bathroom. I casually approached the bathroom when I noticed candles reflecting their light off the mirrors. There must have been fifty or more candles of different sizes spread across the bathroom. The majority of the shimmering lights were around the Jacuzzi. Inside the warm bubbled bath water rested my wife. As she saw me enter the bathroom, she stood up and was wearing a soaked sexy red-laced negligee. The soaked teddy was clinging to her body contouring the beauty of her curves. Any man would have loved this moment, but I was repulsed. I looked at her and lashed out, "What the fuck is this all about? I just got home and I really don't want to have sex or dinner. Get out and let me shower." She stood there in astonishment without saying a word or making a remark. I began to undress and soon afterward began to shower. As I turned off the water and began to towel myself dry, I heard her muffled cries as she lay on our bed. I couldn't understand my behavior, my anger or hatred toward her. I sat on the toilet for several minutes also muffling my sobs confused about who I had become.

It took me a week to call Mario. I again left a detailed message on his voice mail apologizing for my extended delay returning his call. Within thirty minutes, he was returning my telephone call. We spoke for nearly an hour or longer. This time, I asked Mario on a date. He agreed on meeting me for dinner and a movie the next day after work. I told him I was an attorney and lived outside of Miami; therefore, the only time I was able to spend with him was during weeknights after work. I canceled my late afternoon patients and called in sick at my moonlighting job allowing me more time to spend with Monolo after the office. Of course, Maybelle still thought I was working at another office. My first "real" date with a man was wonderful. I knew I was getting into deep water and soon I was going to drown.

Chapter Eight

The time finally arrived. I took Maybelle into the hospital with labor pains on November 30, 1995. On November 29, Maybelle continually *beeped* me throughout the early evening hours. I never called her. I was too involved having sex with Mario and didn't care to call her back. When I arrived home that evening, she told me that she was having mild contractions. I sensed the anger in her tone of voice as she asked me why I didn't call her back. I simply replied, "I was too busy at the office." I measured her contractions and decided they were too far apart to take her into the hospital. I showered and got into bed with her. Caressing her tummy, we both fell asleep. Early morning, on November 30th, her contractions were closer and I decided to take her into the maternity ward. We arrived at Coral Springs Memorial Hospital at about 9 o'clock in the morning where they began to examine her. Unfortunately, her cervix wasn't dilating. If the contractions continued without the cervix dilating, she would have needed a cesarean section. I stayed in the delivery room all day by her side. Luckily, her contraction seized completely for the remainder of the day and evening.

I slept in the hospital that night and by 5 o'clock the next morning Maybelle began contractions again. This time the contractions were closer and more painful. I called the nurse and after examining her she told us that Maybelle's cervix was dilating. The contractions continued and so did the dilation. It wasn't until 11 o'clock in the evening that Maybelle was dilated to seven centimeters. The nurse called the doctor and he arrived fifteen minutes later. It was time. My legs were shaky, my hands trembling and my heart pounding at hundred beats per minutes. I had a myriad of feelings rushing through my body. I was nervous and afraid. I couldn't stand by her side nor coach her breathing pattern. I was too nervous. I decided to stand aside and allow the nurse to aid in the breathing techniques. I simply looked on and watched the pain she was going through birthing my child. Minutes later, the doctor called me to his side where he showed me the crowning. The crowning is the actual head of the child just before delivery. I gave the doctor enough space to be comfortable and I stood to his side while I observed the delivery.

During the entire delivery, I remember praying to God. I never have prayed as much as I did that evening. While Maybelle slept and rested, I would visit the chapel where I would begin the rapport with God. The chapel was small, dark and isolate. I was the only one inside, which allowed me to speak to God aloud without anyone thinking I was crazy. I asked the Creator to give me a healthy child with ten fingers and toes. I recall asking God not to punish my child or me for my promiscuous behavior with men. Lastly, I made a covenant with God. I asked him that if he granted me a healthy and normal child I would discontinue my sexual activities with men. I've always been told not to bargain with God, but for the birth of a healthy child I would have sold my soul to the devil. I made my promises with the best of intentions. I have a considerable amount of faith and truly believed that God would grant me my wishes if I followed through with my promise. How stupid and ignorant I was to think that I was actually going to stop having sex with men.

On December 1, 1995, Alexa-Rae was born. I cried as I held her counting her ten fingers and toes. I held her in my arms for several minutes acknowledging my new life as a father. I was granted a healthy and beautiful baby girl and in return I needed to give up my homosexual life and sexual promiscuity with men.

I hadn't spoken to Mario for several days and was reluctant to call him. However, my anxiety grew stronger and stronger and several days after the birth of my child, I called him. I needed to explain my sudden disappearance and told him I was on a very important business trip and didn't have time to call him. By the sound of his voice, I knew he didn't believe me. Nonetheless, he asked me when we were going to see each other again. I couldn't resist the temptation and despite my promise to God told him I would see him after work the following evening. Our relationship continued much like it was before the birth of my child. When I was with him I forgot about Maybelle, my daughter and even God. I was spending more and more time with Mario and less time at home. We would see each other once or twice a week, but then gradually I would spend every evening with him. Every afternoon, I would drive to Monolo's home and he would have the dinner table ready for me with a lavished entrée. We would have a candle lit dinner every evening and then burn off the calories with incredible sex. It was ironic that I would look forward to my evenings with Mario and not with my family. No matter how bad my day was going at the office, I had him to look forward to in the evenings. Fridays were difficult. I wouldn't see him again until Monday afternoon. I did manage to call him during the weekends, but a telephone call was not the same as having him next to me. I would call him when I walked the dog or from the movie theater while Maybelle sat in the dark auditorium. I would even call him from my den while Maybelle showered or slept. It was even more difficult for him to spend weekends without me. I had my family that kept me busy on Saturdays and Sundays, but he had no one. He didn't have many friends and no family in Miami.

Maybelle was becoming more demanding. She was now dealing with a small infant and a husband that would not arrive home until very late at night. I was arriving later and later every night. Sometimes, Maybelle wouldn't even hear me walk in the house, as she would fall asleep in the nursery while breast-feeding. Mario was becoming more demanding of my time as well. He wanted to spend more time with me, but I simply couldn't. He couldn't understand why I hadn't slept over his apartment. It was several months into our relationship and by now he felt that I should spend some nights over his place. However, I couldn't. He began to get suspicious about my life and questioned me whether I had a lover. Even though I denied it, he wasn't convinced. He gave me an ultimatum. His conditions were that he wanted me to commit more time to him and spend weeknights and weekends together. If I couldn't meet his demands, he would date other men. I became internally irate, but I couldn't blame him. I was jealous knowing that he would share our intimacy with another man. However, I needed to accept it. I had no choice. I was being tugged and pulled by both my wife demanding more time and Mario expecting more from me. The more time I spent with Mario the harder it was to drive home to my wife and child. It was becoming more difficult to leave his home in the evenings and more difficult to stay home on weekends. I knew he was falling in love with me, but he was determined that if I was not committed to our relationship he would have no choice, but to search for the company of other men.

My becoming a father created concreteness into heterosexuality. Even though I was happy in my new role as a father, it created tension within me. After I had the child, I felt that there was no hope in fulfilling my life with a man. In other words, my fatherhood solidified my heterosexuality. My new role as a father and my marriage to Maybelle was a false reality. My life appeared to be real to everyone except me. As my feelings and emotions imprisoned me, I withdrew more from Maybelle and Alexa Rae. I would spend days without holding my daughter or kissing her. I rarely even played with her. I simply didn't want to deal with the notion that I was a father solidified in heterosexuality. I felt lost inside my body. I had no one to turn to. I dealt with my internal demons by creating an emotional isolation between everyone I loved. There were days that I would not speak to anyone except Mario. I would arrive home and say "hello" to Maybelle and ignore Alexa-Rae. I would rush into the shower and retire to bed. Day after day that was my pattern and routine. I continued to harbor the pain for months. My relationship between my family and myself was nonexistent. I saw the pain, anguish and loneliness in Maybelle's face every night when I would arrive home, but did and said nothing to her. My daughter would crawl towards me for a hug and I would walk away. Finally, Maybelle had enough.

Late one evening, she came into the bedroom and began to ask me what was the matter. We spoke briefly about my behavior and I simply told her that I was going through many personal issues. Issues that were too complicated for me to talk to her about. I told her that I was trying to make some resolutions and that the process would take several more weeks and things would eventually be better. She respected my plea and we continued to live separate lives hoping for the resolution I promised her. Of course, several months passed and my family life was still the same. It actually became worse. Alexa Rae was not comfortable around me. As I would reach for her, she would cry and turn to her mother. This only made my isolation from Maybelle and Alexa Rae easier. I began to resent Maybelle for having a child and my child for making me a father. I even resented God. My anger and frustration were projected to those I loved most in my life without realizing I was hurting them. The truth is I was a time bomb. Any moment, I would explode without warning. My situation was volatile and I was not capable of turning off the fuse. I knew that the inevitable was near and the bomb would soon explode.

I was unable to breathe. Choking in my own despair, I knew I needed to leave my family. I couldn't survive any longer in this situation. The time was approaching. I was feeling the anxiety. I was sensing the horror and the pain of telling Maybelle I wanted a separation. I couldn't concentrate at the office. I was having difficulty sleeping and my appetite was totally gone. Even on weekends, I would lay in bed all day long. I had no energy to mow the lawn, clean the pool or make the necessary errands. The thoughts of leaving my family paralyzed my thoughts and body. I knew that Mario was slipping through my fingers and if I didn't act quickly he was going to terminate our relationship. I needed to make a decision quickly about my family life. I needed to make a choice. Mario wanted a commitment and was not waiting any longer and I knew there was no hope for me staying with my family. Hence, the most difficult decision in my life was made.

I chose to leave Maybelle and my child in search of love and companionship with a man. I loved Maybelle, but the yearning for Mario was pulling me away from everything I cherished. I wasn't about to jeopardize my relationship with him and one Friday evening, I decided to sleep over his apartment. It was the first time I slept over a man's apartment. That Friday night my life changed. It was when I decided to throw everything away at home and pursue another life. Mario and I went on a romantic date. He took me to dinner at a small French restaurant in South Beach. After our intimate dinner, we walked Lincoln Road Mall and had Italian ice cream for dessert. It was getting late and I noticed that Mario was becoming melancholy at the thought he would not see me again until Monday night. We drove to his home where we sat on his sofa watching the ten o'clock news. Midway through the newscast, he held my hand and guided me into his bedroom. We stood at the foot of the bed where he and I began to undress each other. Slowly, we undressed enjoying every inch of our exposed flesh. I glanced at the mirrored dresser and saw our bodies in the reflection. Sex was incredible that evening. I sat him on the edge of the bed and continued to remove the remainder of his clothes. We spent endless hours kissing and holding our naked bodies. After several hours of foreplay, he opened his legs and asked me to penetrate him. I obliged. I had rimmed him for several minutes making his ass well lubricated. Gently, I glided my dick inside his body. The warmth I felt all over my own body was sensational. I began to gently and rhythmically thrust my cock inside him. I pulled my dick out and then pushed it slowly inside causing him to moan with ecstasy. It wasn't hard raw sex, but rather soft and tender lovemaking. I was making love for the first time in my life. He looked beautiful. I continued my slow thrusts. Mario asked me to go faster, but I didn't. I wanted the tenderness to last forever. His body was squirming as he moaned from the pleasure he was receiving. After several long and loud moans, I saw his dick begin to ooze white cream on his hairy belly. He pushed himself up toward me and without much struggle laid me on my back. He was now in control. With his knees, he pushed open my thighs forcing permission to penetrate me. He spat several times inside his palm and placed the wet spit on my beckoning ass. He gently and slowly penetrated me and then gradually deepened his manhood inside me. My body was thrusting as never before as I felt his throbbing penis inside me. When he saw my eyes filled with joy, he began to thrust his body towards me. At first, his movements were slow and then stronger and more powerful. Finally, he was pounding me and I was pushing my body toward him allowing him to go deeper inside of me. We created a carefully choreographed and synchronized stage of sexual dance. Within minutes, I shot my load without touching myself and Mario shot his man juice inside me. He leaned over and gently kissed me then whispered, "I love you." We hugged and kissed for several minutes before getting showered.

While bathing each other, I asked him if I would be able to spend the night with him. His eyes lit up like stars in the sky. His smile and the gleam of his eyes meant he accepted my offer. We returned to bed where I held him in my arms until he fell asleep. I gently rolled him to the side of the bed and held him tightly. I began to cry quietly as thoughts of despair and guilt rushed through my mind and heart. While Mario slept, my mind was thinking of what was to come. That Friday, I knew I was not returning home to Maybelle. The feelings that I felt for Mario were enough to make the decision to leave my wife and child. I kept tossing and turning in bed worried about my life, my family and the outcome of my decision. Finally by 4:00 AM, I carefully slipped out of bed and began to dress. Quietly, I took my clothes to the living room where I was able to dress without waking Mario. On a small piece of paper, I wrote Mario a note apologizing for my sudden departure. The note read: *Honey, I am so sorry that I will not awaken next to you in the morning. I am sorry for not holding you until the sun rises, but I needed to go. I will explain why later. Please understand. XOX, Alex.* I left the note on the empty pillow beside him and cautiously walk towards the door of the apartment.

Earlier that evening, I telephoned Maybelle and told her that I would be moonlighting at the hospital's emergency room. I explained to her that

I was helping out a friend that needed the night off. I wasn't concerned of her calling the hospital because it wasn't in her nature to check up on me. However, I did tell her that I would keep the cellular phone on in case she needed to reach me in the event of an emergency. She never called.

It took me nearly an hour to drive home. An hour was not enough time to organize my thoughts, feelings and emotions. I arrived home shortly before six in the morning and decided not to open the garage door. The heavy metal doors created too much noise and possibly could wake Maybelle or Alexa Rae from their sleep. I entered the house through the back and carefully made my way to the bedroom where I undressed. I walked toward the side of the bed and gently sat on the edge of the mattress looking at Maybelle's angelic face as she dreamed. Moments later, her eyes opened and she greeted me with a smile. She must have seen the despair on my face when she asked me what was wrong. I said, "Darling, something is very wrong with me, but we will discuss it when you wake up." I kissed her cheeks and laid my body next to hers. That morning was the last time I held Maybelle in my arms.

Chapter Nine

After several long sleepless hours lying beside her, I began to gently awaken her. Drowsily, Maybelle sat up on the bed and again asked me, "What is wrong with you?" My words were rambled and non-articulated. It was difficult to make sense of my life and more difficult to put it into words. I expressed the hurt and pain I currently was facing dealing with many issues that I didn't know how to resolve. I needed to tell her that I wanted to leave, but I didn't know how. My eyes pooled with tears as I tried to articulate my thoughts and force the words out from my mouth. I kept giving her pieces of a puzzle hoping she could put them together and figure out the whole picture. However, the puzzle was missing too many pieces to create the picture. I was too afraid to tell her straight out that I was leaving her for a man. The innuendoes continued for nearly an hour when I decided to tell her. "Maybelle, I need a separation from you," I told her. "The separation would be temporary. Three months to organize my feelings," I expressed to her. She was shocked. "When? When will you leave?" she asked me. "Today," I replied. Several minutes later, Alexa Rae woke up and Maybelle went to the nursery to tend to my child's needs. The conversation continued, but now with much more emotions in our voices. She was frazzled and confused at the whole morning developments. By 9:30 AM, I was ready to leave everything behind. She looked at me and asked me to promise her I would return. I reached for her and gave her a hug without saying anything. We embraced for endless minutes crying in each other's arms. I turned to Alexa Rae and gave her a kiss good-bye and then turned to Maybelle and said, "Please forgive me for the pain I have caused you all these years. Please don't hate me for who I am or one day will become. I have always loved you and always will." She stood there sobbing as I walked toward the front door. I sat inside my car and looked at the dining room window where Maybelle stood crying and waving good-bye while holding Alexa Rae. I had nowhere to go.

I kept driving until I saw a motel. My first day and night was spent in a small, poorly decorated motel room. I collapsed on the bed early morning and began to cry. No, it was more of a treacherous sob and uncontrollable yelp of anguish that continued for hours. The next day was Sunday. I purchased the newspaper and began my search for apartments. I needed a place quick, so I decided to search the "roommate wanted" section of the classified. I managed to locate three prospects near Maybelle's home, but only one was suitable. It was a two-bedroom condo that would be shared by a heterosexual man. I explained to Erick that I recently separated and needed a place as soon as possible. He was receptive and on Sunday evening I was sleeping in the empty bedroom of Erick's apartment. I slept on the bare carpet without a pillow or anything to cover myself. Monday morning, I telephoned my office and told the administrator that he needed to cancel all my patients until Wednesday. I explained the circumstances to the office manager and he was very kind and supportive making the last minute schedule rearrangements. I showered and decided to drive to my former home to gather my clothes and necessary items.

Maybelle had a very important meeting on Monday morning, which I knew she couldn't cancel, so I headed out to the house early. I entered my house as a guest for the first time. It was empty and void of happiness. There was a thick gloom that lingered in the air. I wondered how Maybelle had slept the night before. I looked around the house as if it was a museum. The walls, furniture and objects of my home were familiar, yet they seemed foreign to me. Trinkets of our travels that I had once cherished now seemed unimportant. As I walked around my former house, it gave me an eerie and uncanny feeling. I continued to walk to the bedroom where I was able to smell the molecules of perfume she wore that morning. Her wet towel laid hanging over one of the pillars of the four-poster bed. I continued my self-guided tour. The bathroom still encompassed the moisture from her early morning shower. Maybelle always made the bed in the mornings. That day she didn't. I sat on the edge of the unmade bed where I began to weep quietly as I looked around my home and smelled her perfume in the air.

I opened my closet door and began to drape shirts with their hangers on my left hand. When the mountain of dress shirts was too much to hold, I took them to the car. Again, I did this until the entire closet was left empty. Shirts, shorts, pants, shoes and everything was put inside my car. "What else do I need?" I asked myself. I went into the guest room and unplugged the television set. Then, I reached over to the bed and grabbed the pillow and comforter that decorated the double bed. Finally, I walked into my den and got a small lamp and alarm clock that rested on my credenza. I unplugged the telephone and placed it inside the cardboard box with the other items. I finished retrieving all my items to begin my new life. I gathered my belongings and began stacking them inside my car. I drove away toward my new apartment with a carload of personal items. After hauling all the clothing and boxes from the car to my new bedroom, I was exhausted. It seemed that I was only able to perform short tasks before requiring sleep. I realized that my extensive energy depletion was depression. I organized my clothes inside my closet and then followed by placing my shoes on the floor of the closet. I put the desk lamp on one corner of the room and spread out the comforter in the middle of the floor with the pillow resting on the wall. The telephone and alarm clock were connected on the other side of the makeshift bed. On the opposite side of the small room, I connected the small 13" television. I laid on the comforter and slowly began to fall asleep. I slept from mid Monday morning until Tuesday morning. Depression makes you sleep for endless hours. I woke up hungry on Tuesday morning and went out for breakfast. After eating, I drove to a nearby grocery store and purchased several items of food. I returned to the apartment where I peacefully began to live my life.

For the next nine months, I lived without a bed or furniture. I simply was not motivated to purchase a mattress to sleep on or furnishings to decorate my room. I didn't need the luxuries of a mattress or furniture. The first day I slept in my apartment I felt a complete and intense internal peace within my body. It seemed that for the first time my guilt was no longer present and my thoughts, feelings and emotions could be felt and processed without guilt or concern for anyone except myself. I was living for the first time in my life and for myself.

Soon after my departure from my family, I met with Mario. He noticed that I was very melancholy and continued to ask me what was wrong. I denied anything to be wrong, but he knew me better. I simply couldn't or didn't want to explain what had occurred several days prior to our meeting. I had no energy or motivation in driving to see Mario. I was simply able to accomplish my necessary daily tasks. I would wake up in the morning, shower, dress, drive to the office, see patients, drive back to the apartment and sleep until the next day. On weekends, I would sleep all day and night. I realized I was falling deeper into a clinical depression. My relationship with Mario was not going well. He had no idea what I was going through and I was not about to explain it either. I was dealing with so much in my life that I just couldn't deal with his demands as well. He was putting more pressure on me than I was able to handle and I decided to end my relationship with him. After meeting him one evening, I expressed my unhappiness and told him I didn't want to see him again. He asked me to give him an explanation, but I didn't. I was relieved that Mario was out of my life. It was too difficult to go through the pain with him. I had to confess my whole life to him and I was not ready for that. I needed to travel this Journey alone.

The first several weeks I would do nothing except go to work and then arrive back to my empty room to sleep. I would sleep for fourteen hours every night and still wake up tired. My appetite was gone, my daily functions were becoming heavy and difficult to perform and I had no motivation to get to the office. I was intelligent enough to acknowledge the symptoms of clinical depression were getting worse and decided to call the local Gay and Lesbian Outreach Center. It took me several days to actually call them after obtaining their phone number. I knew that I would have to explain my circumstances to someone and the "gay" word would eventually be said. I was terrified. Finally, late one evening, I called the Gay and Lesbian Outreach Center hotline.

A man answered the phone. He had a pleasant voice. He seemed older and very soothing. At first, he asked me my name and several general questions. The volunteer then asked me what could he do for me. I briefly explained the reason for my call and that I needed help, but didn't know where to call or whom to call. He put me on hold while he researched several support groups. I was put on hold for several seconds, but it seemed more like hours due to the disturbing silence. There was no pleasant music or a prerecorded message while I waited for his return, but only the sound of my own labored breathing. "Are you still there?" making sure that I had not hung up, he asked. "Yes," I replied. It was difficult to respond to him through my quivered voice as tears rolled down my face. He began to ask me several more questions until his digging created a hole in my soul. I began to sob uncontrollably and he just stayed listening to the absence of articulation. After several minutes, the soft-spoken man referred me to a gentleman that was the facilitator of a support group for married gay men in the "coming out" process. Through his soothing talk, the strange voice managed to alleviate my pain temporarily. I wrote down the telephone number of Greg, the facilitator of the married men's group, thanked the volunteer and hung up the telephone. I called Greg that same evening and he gave me the information concerning the meeting of the group. Greg appeared to be very concerned about me and managed to call me every night until the eve of the meeting. We spoke briefly every day giving me the needed boost of energy to continue living into the next day.

No one knew of our separation. Neither my parents nor hers were aware of our problems. Both our parents thought we had the prefect marriage (and so did everyone else). My Mom, Dad and friends still thought I was living at home. Maybelle didn't even know my whereabouts for the first couple of days. I called her voice mail several days after my move giving her my new telephone number. She called me that same night and we spoke about what to say to the family. I told her that I would discuss the issue soon with my family and she could do the same with hers. I don't know what she told her parents nor did I care, but I was nervous on how to break the news to my parents. I decided to discuss the issue with my brother first. I called his house late one evening while he and his wife were in bed and told them I needed to discuss something of utmost importance. My brother offered his ear and I drove to their home that same night. I broke the news to them quickly. They were surprised, but confused because I gave them no reason why I had made such a decision to leave my family and home. They asked me whether there was another woman. I said, "No." "Then what?" my brother asked me. I said nothing. I simply expressed to them that I couldn't be married to her any longer. My brother expressed his love and support, but was still dumbfounded at why I made such a decision to leave Maybelle. Thanking them for their time, I drove back to my empty room. My next step was my parents. I called my Mom and Dad several days later and explained what had occurred between Maybelle and myself. After much discussion and questions, they expressed their love and support for me.

I arrived early to the "Coming Out" group. In the lobby of the building, a poster stood on an easel posting the evening's meetings. The meeting was scheduled to start at seven o'clock in room 212. It was only 6:40 PM. I was early. I went upstairs and began to walk in search of room 212. The door was closed, but not locked. I went inside the small room where I sat around a large oval table. There were fifteen chairs around the table. I wondered whether all the seats would be occupied with men in similar circumstances. There was nothing else except the table and chairs in the room. I sat in my chair nervous and afraid until slowly I began to relax. Moments later, the other individuals began arriving. The last person to arrive was the facilitator of the group, Greg. He introduced himself and instructed the attendees to briefly say something about themselves. I was the last person to introduce myself to the group. I told the other members that I was extremely depressed and lonely due to recently leaving my wife and child. I never mentioned why I decided to leave my wife because it should have been obvious from my participation in the group. Some of the members of the group asked me if I had any gay friends and of course my reply was, "No." Within seconds, a list was made up with everyone's name and telephone numbers. I instantly had a network of friends that shared many of my problems. Some of the men had children. Others, were divorced and in search of a male partner. While a handful of the men, were still married and living double lives.

Driving home after the meeting, I felt I had made a significant progress. I had someone to talk and express my pain and feelings about my life. I had friends that shared similar life experiences and could feel comfortable telling them about my secret life. The group was composed of mostly middle-aged men and one woman. The men and woman were relatively closeted and not into the bars or traditional gay scene. I was the youngest of the group. My telephone, soon after the initial meeting, wouldn't stop ringing. Every man in the group was calling me giving me the support and conversation I desperately needed. Within days, I had made new friends that shared similar interests and common emotional struggles. My nights and weekends were busy being entertained by my new group of friends.

With my new friends, came a new set of problems into my life. It wasn't long after meeting my friends when I understood their ulterior motives. I realized that my new acquaintances were more interested in *bedding* me than helping me through my pain. I was rather innocent when it came to acknowledging their sexual innuendoes; hence, their insistence proved successful. I decided to take the bait. I had sex with nearly half the men in the group. It took me two or three weeks to accomplish the sexual task of sleeping with most of the members. Afterwards, I felt more empty and weaker emotionally. I stopped attending the meetings and was left alone once again. No one from the group called me after exchanging sexual pleasures. They simply used me to satisfy their own sexual needs.

The time spent with these men allowed me to practice my skills. The skills of sex. Without knowing, I was becoming an expert in giving pleasure. Sexual pleasure, that is. For some unexplained reason, my own insecurities were relieved when I gave these men pleasure. In the brief moments I exchanged in sexual favors, I felt strong and powerful, but then weak and empty afterwards. Much like an alcoholic feels pouring a drink into his/her veins. Alcoholics consume the alcohol because it makes them feel good, strong and powerful. He/she continues to feel invincible in their state of intoxication, but as he/she sobers they become weak and *strengthless*. I was proud that every man would tell me they had never been with someone as good as me. I, for the first time, became visible in a population. I was no longer the six-grade *faggot* that no one would pick for the football team. I became a sex jock.

Meanwhile, I was still dealing with my secret. I would speak to Maybelle on a daily basis telling her that I was working on my issues. She was confident that our lives would resume to normal shortly. I wasn't that positive. Maybelle and I made arrangements to "date" each other while separated. She felt the dates would rekindle our love once again. We would go out to dinner or a movie, but it just didn't feel right. I would drive her back to her home and then drive myself to my empty apartment. There were nights that we were intimate, but it wasn't because I wanted or had the urge to have sex with her. It was simply to prove to her that I could still sexually function as a man. She was confused at my enigmatic life, but patient nonetheless. I wasn't as patient. My yearning for men was becoming more powerful every day.

In many conversations I had with Maybelle, the topic of sexuality came up. I remember one evening that we were lying on the floor of my room when she began to give me a blowjob. My dick didn't respond to the oral gratification and she was dumbstruck. I was nervous at my own unresponsiveness and she then proceeded with the questions. "Are you gay?" she asked. "Or, bisexual?" she added. I answered, "No" to both questions. By then, I knew the truth. I was fully aware I was *queer*, but I was too afraid to tell her. I was too fearful of the ramifications of telling someone (especially my wife) that I was gay. However, it would only be a matter of days before she discovered the truth.

I still had not step foot into a gay bar and it would be several months before I would open the door of a gay bar and walk myself inside. However, I needed to meet men. I was in search of finding a man. I didn't realize that I was not emotionally ready to meet anyone, but I still wanted to have sex with men. So, I needed another avenue (other than a gay bar) to meet men. I came across a "find a date" telephone line from the local newspaper. It was a line that with a prepaid charge account you would call and hear messages from other callers or record your own personal message. There were several categories to choose from in the prerecorded menu. For example: *Gay and Looking for Quick Sex, Gay and Looking for LTR, Married Men that Like Men* and *Bisexuals* were only some of the many categories of the "351 Line." I don't know why it was called the "351 Line", but that was the name. The first several times I called I would respond only to the bisexual category ads leaving my contact information and brief message to the anonymous masculine voices. I would give them a brief description of myself and tell them I was bisexual. I simply COULD NOT say I was gay. After the men would hear my description, they would call me and we would eventually meet. It was similar to a match making service, but with a slight twist. Appearance and looks was not important. I wanted sex and nothing else from the men I met. The match making service wasn't free. It was costing me a *pretty penny* to meet these men for sex, but with my American Express I was able to get hours of credit with the company. However, what I didn't realize was that my mail was still being delivered to Maybelle's home. One day, she decided to open the American Express statement and examine the charges. This is when she discovered the truth. She called the credit card company and asked for the telephone number of the charges that appeared under "Telecommunication Network." She called and discovered her husband was spending much of his time and money enjoying other men's company with the aid of a gay matchmaking service.

The same night she discovered my secret she confronted me. She surprised me by showing up at my apartment with the American Express statement in her hand. She demanded an explanation, but I had none. I simply looked at her and said nothing. I didn't try to cover-up the charges nor lie. I stayed quiet. This was when she ousted me. She was irate and irrational. She was confused and hurt. I still remember the pain of her face as she cried when she discovered the truth about her husband's life. There was no turning back now. I pleaded with her not to tell anyone. I asked her to keep my secret silent from my parents' preventing the unnecessary pain and disappointment the revelation of their son's identity would have on them. She did avoid telling my parents, but everyone else found out quickly. The friends I had when married soon turned their back on me and her family that once loved me now demonstrated anger at their ex-son-in-law. Maybelle's anger grew as quick as cancer. Her anger was overpowering her life and mine. It was difficult for her to understand that I was gay and even more difficult to understand that the marriage she once had could have been a deception from the beginning. I continually reassured her that my love for her was true, but she didn't want to understand. To this date, Maybelle's anger prevents her from moving forward in her life. Struggling with my own issues, I was determined to move forward in my life and search for who I was and where I was going in my Journey.

I met several men on the "351 Line." Some of these men have impacted my life and continue to be close friends and others were simply used for my sexual pleasures. One such encounter was Ted. He introduced himself as an attorney and was currently married, but not having sex with his wife. Ted seemed well adjusted at his secret lifestyle. He was professional, well educated and articulate with his words. He was handsome, but a bit on the chunky side. Nonetheless, he seemed like a good fuck and I was horny. We met on several occasions, but after several dates I began to have difficulty with his matrimonial situation. He was not ready to let go of his wife and I wasn't ready to date someone with a wife. After several secret sexual encounters, I decided not to see him again. Ted and I didn't speak for several months. One afternoon, he called me at the office and we resumed where we had left off, but this time as friends.

Several years later, Ted is still in status quo. He is still in a sexless marriage and continues his search for happiness. Several years after we met, I found out that Ted was not a successful attorney, but an impoverished paralegal. Despite the lies and untruths, I have managed to keep a good friendship with him. I realize that Ted has many issues and will probably never arrive to resolve any of the multitude of personal problems due to his self-hatred and lack of self-acceptance.

I met several other men on the "351 Line." All the men had many more issues than myself and I needed to let them go. For instance, Larry was a very beautiful man. He was *closeted* and hated himself for being gay. After sexual intercourse, he would begin to feel extremely guilty and tell me that God would punish us for our behavior. If I am not mistaken, he actually said, "The Lord will have no mercy on us. Fornication is a sin and we will suffer the consequences of the wrath of God." He was a religious fanatical *nut*. Sometimes, he would quote the Bible verses aloud while having sex. Other times, he would kneel on the floor and pray an "Our Father" or "Hail Mary." One evening in his self-hatred, he began to pray and ask God for forgiveness. While in his rapport with God, he called himself a sinner and fornicator. I watched in astonishment as he continued in his religious self-pity. However, the scene took another turn when I heard him tell God that I was also a sinner and fornicator and needed to be guided by the Lord. I had heard enough bullshit! I was outraged as I heard him call me a sinner and fornicator. I jumped off the bed and helped him off his knees. I had enough guilt of my own and didn't need Larry's religious convictions to make me feel worse. Needless to say, I never saw him again. I won't be surprised if he became a Roman Catholic priest.

Finally, I met Carl. He was average looking with a muscular body. We began to date and soon ended up sexually involved. I soon entered into the world of sadism and masochism. I had no idea the pain this guy enjoyed. I was inexperience in this realm of sexual pain and kink, but soon mastered all the techniques. I became bored and after learning all I wanted to learn from him, it was time to move on.

I became bored meeting people on the phone line. I had nothing to hide as many of these men did. Many were ugly and couldn't meet anyone in a bar. Some were married to women and couldn't actively go out to a gay club and a few were in relationships and simply liked to fuck around. Others were religious freaks that wanted to self-mutilate themselves with guilt and pity. I had no need to hide and felt that the phone line was not my cup of tea.

The anger brewed stronger in Maybelle's soul towards me. She had (and still has) a difficult time letting go of her marriage, her husband and the life she dreamed of having with me. She prevented me from visiting my daughter and took all possible measures to make my life a living hell. Still today, I have to deal with Maybelle's rage towards me. I have always been pleasant to her insults and never attacked her verbally despite all the irrational behavior she demonstrated. I understood her anger, frustration and despair, but I continued to strive to make my life whole and complete with or without her approval or kindness.

Through a gay friendly newspaper, I saw the advertisement of a gay bar. I had no friends to call and escort me, but that never stopped me. I knew that my presence in a gay bar was a big step and needed to go no matter what. I was nervous and afraid of what I would encounter in the tavern, but made a choice to face my fears and visit the establishment. Whom I might see and who might see me in the bar were two of my worries, but I managed to get inner strength and one evening I drove to Cathode Ray. I parked my car in a back alley near the rear entrance of the bar. For twenty minutes, I watched as other men entered the bar. Some seemed to enter through the front door, but others chose the more discrete rear entrance. For me, it would be the back entrance. I began to walk toward the back door. My heart was pounding and legs weak, as I strolled toward the door.

A man wearing leather pants and vest opened the door and I entered the establishment. It was dark and smoky causing me difficulty to discern the three steps in front of me. I stumbled over the concrete steps and someone helped me off my feet. I felt foolish and wanted to turn around and leave. I asked myself, *What was I doing here?* I continued to walk upstairs as if I was a frequent patron of the bar and knew exactly where to go. I made my way to the bar counter where I stood for several minutes with poise and confidence creating a facade of self-assurance. However, deep below the facade I was nervous. I looked around and had never seen so many men of "my kind" in one place. The majority of the men were beautiful. These men were nothing like the guys from the Turnpike plazas, shopping malls or the "351 Line." I was in awe at the beauty around me. I don't drink, but decided I needed to drink to loosen up a bit. I felt that a drink or two would reduce my nervousness and allow me to mingle with the crowd. I ordered a *Screwdriver,* a mixture of vodka and orange juice. The tall thin glass of yellow fluid went down like water. I then ordered a second and then a third and finally a forth. I was certainly feeling better as the yellow fluid raced through my veins. It became easy to stare at men and soon afterwards they were approaching me. How simple this seemed. Was it the vodka or my looks or both that made this seem so simple? I was blessed (or maybe cursed) at having such ease and charm with men.

My first night at Cathode Ray I went home with someone. I can't remember his name, but it was wonderful. Soon afterwards, I became a regular patron at Cathode Ray. It became easier and easier to enter through the door of the bar and soon I was visiting the smoky dark tavern nightly. It didn't take me very long to create a rather *whorish* reputation for myself. The rumors didn't stop me. I simply would go to a new bar and start sleeping with most men there as well. I would have sex every day of the week. Sometimes, I would meet a guy and bring them home then I would return to the bar for more sexual prey. It seemed to me that I was making up for lost time. I was out of control.

Every night different bars offered nightly themes. For example, Mondays were *Beer Bash Mondays* at Cathode Ray, Tuesdays were *TV Tuesdays* at Boots, Wednesdays were *Men of Power* at Electra, Thursdays were *Long Island Ice Tea* at Georgie's Alibi, etc. On Wednesdays, I would go to Electra where it was packed with men. It was a dance club rather than a neighborhood bar. It was in this dance club I met Harry.

He was older than myself (much older) and seemed to know my insecurities well. He bought me a drink from across the bar and I then approached him thanking him for the gesture. He complimented me on everything from my smile to my looks and body to my *bulge*. Needless to say, I went home with him that evening. As I walked inside his beautiful oceanfront home, someone else was waiting. It was another man. Both men handed me some poppers and they began to undress me. Harry and the other man were in their fifties, but well preserved. They were slow and meticulous removing my clothes making the pleasure of their hands touching my body explosive. The men appeared to be more like animals than humans as their mouths drooled for my body. In the background, music played giving me permission to perform for them. They sat on the sofa salivating as they watched their prized dinner dancing for them. My dick was hard as a rock. Harry and his friend didn't necessarily sexually excite me, but the pleasure I was giving them was enough to make my dick explode. The more they lusted over my body the more explosive the yearning to please them. I straddled Harry's friend on the sofa while reaching for Harry's crotch giving them the pleasure they deserved. Their heartbeats were raising and droplets of sweat trickled down the sides of their faces as they continued to lust for my body. I began to remove their clothing exposing the fur of gray hair on their chests and stomachs. My hand was massaging Harry's dick as I straddled his friend on the sofa. Harry's friend was moaning with ecstasy as my hard cock rested on his belly. The moaning and grunting became louder and fierce. Harry stood up and came behind me on the sofa. He held me tight with his two hands around my waist and without warning penetrated me. I opened my legs wider while still squatting over his friend allowing deeper entry into my ass. Then, the unexpected happened. Harry's friend reached for his dick and began to search for my hole as well. Both men were inside me at the same time. Rhythmically, I began to thrust allowing both men to feel the tightness of my ass. The moaning continued louder and louder until the man below me ejaculated. Moments later, Harry did the same. That night I don't remember myself *cumming*. It has always been difficult for me to *cum* under the influence of alcohol and poppers.

For some unknown reason, I felt strong and powerful. Not sick and disgusted, but content in being extremely talented sexually. I reached over for my jeans and pulled them up to my waist. They asked me to stay for a glass of wine and I agreed. I followed Harry to the kitchen where I was handed a glass of white wine. I began to sip from the crystal goblet as he guided me to the outside patio where the swimming pool was located. I rolled my jean legs up several inches and draped my legs over the side of the pool. The water was cold, but soothing nonetheless. He sat behind me massaging my neck and back while he proceeded to ask me questions. "What do you do for a living?" he asked. I told him I was a medical student. Of course, I lied. I was already a practicing physician. "Your parents help you financially?" he asked. "No," I answered. "It must be tough?" Harry remarked. "At times," I replied. He then asked me if I wanted to work for him. "Doing what?" I asked with inquisitiveness. His reply shocked me, "As a male escort," he said. Harry continued with the job description telling me that I would strip dance at a bar he owned in town and then hustle men afterwards. "Partial proceeds will come to me and you will take home the rest," he added to his illustrative job description. I remained expressionless as I turned my head toward him. I smiled and told him it was time for me to go. I went inside and retrieved my other garments and headed toward the front door. I waved good-bye to his friend and continued toward the foyer. Before opening the door, I turned to Harry to say good-bye when he handed me three hundred dollars. "This is how much you are worth for the pleasure you gave us tonight," he said softly. I took the money and continued walking outside to my car. *Three hundred bucks,* I thought to myself, *for being such a novice. Not bad. Not bad at all.*

Chapter Ten

After little consideration, I took up Harry's offer. During the day, I was a successful doctor and in the evenings, a stripper and male escort. On weekends, I was a part-time caring father. What turmoil I had fallen myself into. I was on a path of destruction. It was a road that led me to self-hatred and emptiness months later. I continued to dance for several months, but my true love was the "sex-for-pay" industry.

After performing my dance routine, I would make my rounds on the floor looking for hungry men. Most evenings were profitable, but some were slow. Harry was always surrounded by beautiful men and his friends were well aware of the entourage of boy studs that were hungry and eager for extra income. He was a businessman and needed to make his profits even on the slow nights; therefore, he would arrange off duty jobs for me with affluent individuals that would pay for private entertainment. He assigned me to both men and women, but my preference was men. Despite the beauty of the women I "dated", I enjoyed giving pleasure to men more. I continued to dance, hustle and escort in the evenings and then work at my office in the mornings. My life became exhausting, yet exhilarating. Harry realized I was more profitable to him as an escort than a dancer, so he decided to reassign me to his escorting side business full-time. Harry would call me at home and arrange one or two clients for the night. He would not let me rest. I was hustling seven days a week making both of us plenty of money. Money, by the way, I didn't need. He would briefly describe my clients as, "Professional, fifties, fat and ugly, wants to top, likes to get rimmed. He's a good client so treat him special." He then offered suggestions on how to dress and where to meet the client. Then, he described my second client for the evening.

The women I "dated" were beautiful and affluent. They were old, but still carried themselves with much distinction and beauty. I enjoyed my evenings considerably with them. They would take me to elaborate functions, expensive dinners and very nice trips. The men, on the other hand, were much cheaper. At times, I would "date" a man that wanted to treat me well and acquire a boy toy for their personal use and pleasure. Most of the times, it was hard and raw sex absent of conversations or intimacy.

Albert became a frequent client of mine. He was a tall and handsome retired US Army 2nd Lieutenant. He had the grace and charm of a true gentleman. Albert was more than thirty years my senior, but his age was no concern to me. The more I "dated" him the more I enjoyed his company and him mine. Harry wasn't fond of clients that would monopolize one of his boys; therefore, he would reluctantly assign me to Albert every time I was requested. Albert and I began to establish a close friendship and one evening while on a "date" he made a proposition. He wanted me to move in with him. In addition to the free room and board, I would earn a substantial weekly salary and as a bonus an automobile. I still don't know why I considered his offer or why I moved in with him, but I did. Previously, I had mentioned to him that I was a medical student and couldn't spend the days with him. I also told him that many of my nights were spent in the library studying; however, I would return to him in the evenings giving the pleasure he needed and was financially paying. The arrangement gave me the time I needed to work at my office and spend time with my daughter without him discovering my true identity. After the business deal was mutually agreed upon, he handed me the keys to his spare car. The vehicle was a silver colored Mercedes Benz CLK convertible Kompressor. Within days, I had my clothes and belongings hanging from the large walk-in closet in his bedroom. The entire scenario reminded me of a movie I once saw, *Pretty Woman* starring Julia Roberts, where a prostitute falls in love with a millionaire and lives happily ever after. Unfortunately, such romances only occur in movies.

My relationship with Albert was kept a secret. It was understood that Harry did not appreciate any of his boys to move in with his clients because it would financially disturb his income flow. Therefore, I kept my relationship secret from my friends and Harry. Several days after moving in with Albert, I called Harry to inform him that I wanted to retire from the "sex-for-pay" industry. He sadly let me go, but not without much persuasion in the form of financial bonuses. However, my decision was made. Albert treated me very well and I enjoyed a very lavished lifestyle in the Islands of Miami Beach. We would spend the evenings together enjoying each other's company while I gave him the pleasure he demanded and expected. Unfortunately, the fun didn't last long. It didn't take long before he got bored in our monogamous relationship and began to bring other boys home.

Several times a week, we would have three-ways or four-ways with other beautiful boys. However, one evening things got out of hand. Albert always supplied his *boy bitches* with lots of drugs. This evening he too got wasted and insisted for the other boys to gang fuck me. I had no objections to his request, but he wanted them to fuck me *bare back* and I refused. That evening he threw me out of his home. I turned over his car keys and called a cab. I loaded the taxi with three Hefty bags of my personal belongings. Albert was my last and only *sugar daddy*. I felt it was too difficult to juggle my professional life and daughter with a permanent sugar daddy. This would have been the perfect time to change my life, but I didn't. I was addicted to sex and men.

My life continued to be secretive. My few friends, my family and Maybelle knew nothing about my sexual escapades. I would avoid visiting or speaking to my parents because I was afraid they might discover their son was a paid whore. The drugs and excessive sleepless nights were making me look tired and worn out, but I continued. I continued on the path of self-destruction. I began to hustle again one week after leaving Albert. This time I went solo that meant I needed to make my own "dates" and set my own fees. It also meant that all the profits went inside my pocket. I began to call old clients and soon had a busy and booming business, but this time without a pimp.

I would usually have one or two "dates" scheduled per night, but some evenings were slow. I would come home from the office and have a light dinner. I would then head out to the gym for a one-hour workout. After my heated gym workout, I would shower. While lathering, I felt my body get antsy, yearning for sexual excitement. I ached for the fix of sex and men. If I had no "dates" scheduled, I would hustle the streets of Fort Lauderdale until a "date" picked me up. I couldn't charge my usual fee in the streets, so my fees were *a la carte*. I would charge twenty bucks for blowjobs, thirty-five dollars to top someone or fifty bucks to bottom. Most of my "dates" were pure vanilla, but some wanted kink, which made my financial profits greater. I would pick up seven to ten "dates" per night usually for quick blowjobs inside their car or at a nearby park. It wasn't the money that kept me in the hustling lifestyle, but the disease of my addiction.

There were several hustlers around my *zone* that soon became my buddies. Being an independent hustler is dangerous; therefore, buddies were a necessity to stay alive. We weren't taken care of by a pimp and sometimes we would pick up some sick mother fucker that was out to beat the shit out of us. Needless to say, we all took care of each other. My *bitch boy* (as we called each other) buddies were severely emotionally fucked up. Actually, the majority of them were straight, but hustled men for their drug habits. Some were teenagers that were thrown out of their homes for being gay. I, on the other hand, was simply a sex addict that hustled the streets for my nightly fix. I was shocked at how dirty and filthy they appeared, but regardless of their appearance and body odor, they managed to make money hustling the streets and parks of Ft. Lauderdale. Most of them slept in the park and the junkies slept anywhere they happened to end up that night. We all had our own territorial zone called *The Zone*. We knew better not to *trick* anywhere near someone else's turf or *zone*. I worked my turf and they worked theirs. I respected them and they respected me. The streets were dangerous. Knife attacks, beatings and shootings were commonly heard about. Luckily, I never encountered anything of that sort. It is interesting that I was not afraid to get murdered as much as I was to get arrested by the Ft. Lauderdale Police Department. You can only imagine how the newspaper headlines would read. I honestly would have rather been dead than arrested. Fortunately, neither occurred. Quick blowjobs in the park never scared me, but car "dates" always were frightening. I never managed to shake off the fear as I entered a "date's" car. I thought to myself I would one day get a knife pierced through my back as I was *going down* on a *trick*. Luckily, it never happened. I rather have "dated" men that were referred by someone else than hustled the streets, but when you are an addict it doesn't matter how or where you get the fix as long as you get it. This was my situation.

During my tormented adolescence, I lacked self-esteem and self worth. In my mind, I was worth nothing. While hustling, I felt powerful and strong. In my "sex-for-pay" world, I was significant and important to someone. Men would want me for my body not for who I pretended to be. I catered to all their needs and wants. I created a scene that no other hustler would come close in matching. I wanted to be the best and I became the best in giving my clients pleasure. I entered my clients' minds and transformed their weaknesses into power while giving me the pseudo self-worth I searched for in my own life. If they were timid, I made them assertive. If they lacked self-esteem, I made them self-assured. I would play the sex game with expertise and ease. I would enter their bodies and minds creating a world that no one had created for them before. Their minds were my playground and their body my playmate. I was as serious about my evening career as I was when examining my patients at the office. I wanted to be the best hustler as well as the best physician. I was both.

Most of these men were old and physically unattractive. They were affluent and wanted someone young, good looking and physically fit to give them pleasure. It became very difficult for me to perform for these clients as "Alex"; therefore, I created another identity. His name was Jon. Jon was my other personality. He encompassed who and what I have never been. He was the whore and slut that Alex couldn't be. He was strong, self assured and confident. Jon was whom I always wanted to be, but couldn't. He had the assertiveness and high self-esteem that Alex lacked. Mentally, I would transform myself into Jon before heading out to meet a client or hustle the streets. At first, the metamorphosis was difficult to accomplish, but it didn't take long before Jon would come easily into existence. It also didn't take long before I enjoyed Jon more than Alex. He was becoming more a part of my life and I enjoyed his attributes and self-assurance. Finally, through my search for happiness and recovery from my sexual addiction both Jon and Alex united to form who I am today.

It was difficult to perform some sexual pleasures with some men; however, I always managed to overcome my scruples. Even if they were obese and wanted me to rim their sweaty hole, I did. I became a bottom for the tops and a top for the bottoms. I would role-play and perform kink without hesitation. I practiced *water sports* and *scat*. I did everything and anything for these men. While assuming the persona of Jon, I was lost in the moment of sexual play. However, upon payment for my services, I began to come down from my *high*. As Jon would begin to disappear and Alex would return, I quickly would encounter a void and emptiness within me. I would sometimes drive home hating myself, my parents, and all the six graders and everyone that hurt me as a child. I would arrive home and scrub myself clean. I would vigorously scrub as a rape victim does after the act of violence was perpetrated. I would crawl into bed crying myself to sleep wondering what I was doing to my life. The majority of the money earned from my escorting and hustling was donated to various organizations. I gave to AIDS organizations, gay churches and one day gave $100.00 bills to several homeless men on my way home from a "date." The money was not important to me. I made decent money as a physician and didn't need to supplement my income nor moonlight. I did what I was doing because I was sick.

I recall one afternoon getting a page from a client. He identified himself as a forty-five year old professional man that was interested in meeting me. Someone he mentioned, which I couldn't recall, recommended me. He went on to say, "Our meeting must be discreet. I'm married." After a brief conversation, I told him I would meet him at a hotel in South Beach. I told him the usual, "The fee for the service is $175.00 cash only." I continued by saying, "Anything goes, but if you want kink it will cost more." He agreed to everything I said and then gave him further instructions, "Register yourself in the hotel and *beep* me with the room number. I would then go to your room." I had just come from the gym and quickly showered. I left my home about one hour after our conversation. I arrived at the hotel just when the client *beeped* me with room number 309. I went up the stairs and knocked at the door. Within seconds, he opened the door. He was taller then myself with a slender, but toned muscular body. His hair was dark with salt and pepper specks along the temples. He was dressed in navy blue dress pants and a white Perry Ellis shirt with a gold colored business tie. As he opened the door, I looked at him and recognized who he was. He was a colleague that frequented the same conferences I did. I had seen him several times at different functions and lectures; however, it appeared he didn't recognize me. It was difficult to fathom even if he did recognize me that a doctor would be a male escort. Also, I dressed rather frumpish. For instance, that day I wore old jeans with some rips and holes and a short sweater vest. My jeans were worn low giving him a glimpse of my Calvin Klein underwear. The short sweater vest allowed my *pecs* and biceps to show nicely. He never looked at my face. He wouldn't stop looking at my body, but never my face. I led myself inside the room and he offered me a glass of wine. "No, thank you," I replied. Time was money and I had no time to waste by sipping wine or engaging in bullshit conversation. As he was pouring the wine, I stood behind him and began to kiss his neck. He began to moan and then I turned his body towards me. I continued to work him completely until I felt his hard-on through his dress pants. I undressed myself and remained in my Calvin Klein underwear. He clumsily began to do the same. I got the intuition he liked to get fucked, so I became the aggressor. He seemed nervous, so I poured him another glass of wine. After his second glass of wine, he was more relaxed. I gave him pleasure for forty-five minutes licking him all over his hairy body. His eyes were closed as he moaned from the pleasure I was giving him. We were still standing and he was still holding the second glass of wine. I removed the glass from his hand and placed the wine glass on the desk. I leaned him over the desk chair and began to eat his hairy asshole. As I opened his butt cheeks to expose his sphincter, his moans became louder giving me permission to fuck him. His asshole was wet with spit and I then began to finger his tight and begging hole. Gradually, I would poke one, then two and finally three fingers deep inside his asshole. He was moaning as a woman does when she's getting fucked. The more I fingered his hole the more his legs opened inviting me inside. I told him to hold his butt cheeks wide allowing me more freedom for my four fingers to enter. At first, I was finger-fucking him slowly, but then I began to penetrate his ass faster giving him more painful pleasure. I guided him to the edge of the bed where I laid him on his back. I then propped a pillow under his hip making it easier for my dick to enter his hairy man hole. Then, I penetrated him. I taught myself not to *cum* and would be able to thrust for endless hours. I practiced this technique in case I had other "dates" the same evening. He was in pure ecstasy. He kept telling me he was "close" and in my final thrust he grabbed his dick. With three quick strokes, he was shooting his semen all over himself. He squirted his white man-juice well passed his head and slowly the squirts then reached his chest and lastly his hairy stomach. I took some *cum* between my thumb and index finger and began to feed it to him. He asked me if I had *cum* and of course I lied and told him, "Yes." We dressed and he paid my fee with a twenty-five dollar tip.

I left the hotel room in a daze. I couldn't believe that this client was a colleague. If he had recognized me, my career would have been over. Nonetheless, I laughed it off. I was certain that even if he recognized me he would not mention the incident to anyone. I continued my drive home to rest for a busy day at the office the following morning. Several months later, I sat in the row behind him in Orlando, Florida at a conference. Needless to say, he never acknowledged me.

I got to the point in my life that I needed help. I recognized that my disease was controlling my life. The drugs, alcohol and late night "dates" were creating havoc in my office. I was having difficulty staying alert and awake while at the office and I was falling deeper into a clinical depression. My life was in turmoil. I needed to talk to someone.

Thumbing through the *Gay Yellow Pages* for a therapist, I came across his advertisement. His quarter-page ad mentioned he specialized in "Gay issues, Couples and Addiction." I was gay and I was also an addict. He seemed to be the perfect man for the job. I called the seven-digit telephone and reached his answering service. I left a message for him to call me as soon as possible. The woman taking the message asked me, "Is this an emergency?" I said, "YES!" Within thirty minutes, the doctor was calling me back. I'll call him Dr. Scum for obvious reasons that will be illustrated later on. After introducing himself, I explained my situation. He mentioned that he was booked, but due to my depression he would see me the following day at 8:00 PM.

I arrived at Dr. Scum's office thirty minutes early. I opened the main door to his office and approached the glass window and rang the bell. I sat and waited. Several minutes later, Dr. Scum opened the office door and introduced himself. I followed him through a long hallway and entered the last office. He sat behind a large Mahogany desk and I sat opposite him. He was in his late forties and relatively handsome. He appeared to be stoic and poised behind his desk creating a persona of professionalism. He began to ask me questions and jotting notes on a yellow legal pad. Candidly, I answered all his questions. At the end of the session, he expressed genuine concern and interest in pursuing the case.

I began to see progress after my fourth and fifth therapy, but on the sixth session something happen. Ten minutes before the sixth session ended, Dr. Scum came behind me and began to massage my neck. I found his behavior inappropriate, but allowed him to continue. After several minutes of kneading my neck muscles, his hands began to migrate down-ward to my chest. I was shocked at first, but said and did nothing. His hands continued to move downward. He moved the swivel chair to face him. Actually, I was at eye level with his crotch. It was then my turn. I unzipped his pants and exposed his hard cock. I sucked his dick for several minutes until he shot his load inside my mouth. Needless to say, the sub-sequent therapy sessions were delivered at no charge. I simply needed to give him a blowjob at the end of each session. In other words, his fees were the blowjobs I was providing. I stopped showing up to my weekly appointments, which made him very concerned and worried. He was pet-rified that I would report his unethical behavior to the Department of Professional Regulations. It wasn't worth my time and effort to do such a thing.

I soon realized that no matter where I turned or whom I reached out for help they would take advantage of me. I was emotionally vulnerable and people knew how to press the right buttons to get their needs met through me. While individuals were meeting their needs, I was left empty, lonely and more emotionally fucked up. I believed that no one would help me except myself. I made a choice to be my own teacher, guide and thera-pist striving to get better emotionally. What I needed to do was a consid-erable amount of soul searching and self-analysis trying to find the right path to take in my Life Journey.

I took one day at a time. Slowly, I was taking control of my life again. I was noticing that "dates" would call me and I would not show up. Sometimes, it was difficult to masquerade my true feelings of disgust and emptiness while performing with a "date." There were other instances that when I did show up to meet a *trick*, I was unable to sexually perform. Some of the clients would get violently upset at my lack of sexual enthusi-asm. In one instance, a man ordered me to give him an enema. My "date" handed me an enema bottle and instructed me to insert the soapy solution into his rectum. Then, he wanted me to insert a butt plug in his asshole brewing the fecal matter inside his intestinal walls. Afterwards, he would squat over me and pull the black butt plug expelling the brown, soapy shit-laced water all over me. He was a repeat customer and I had performed this scene on two separate occasions, but that night I wanted no part in his kinky fetish. After refusing his request, he became violent. He got physically aggressive and moments later, he had me pinned against the hotel bathroom's sink. He told me he had no time to waste and would "beat the shit out of me" if I didn't do as he wished. Still pinned against the sink, I reached for his throat with my right hand. Firmly squeezing his throat, I pushed him back against the bathroom wall. I continued to compress his windpipe while softly whispering in his ear, "Don't ever threaten me again, mother fucker." Five seconds more and I would have suffocated the bastard. I relaxed my hand from his throat and he fell on the bathroom tiled floor gasping for air. While I got dressed, he continued to gasp and cough catching bits of the air he so desperately needed. I reached for his wallet and took out two $100.00 bills. I ripped the two bills into tiny pieces and threw the green confetti at him. He looked up at the floating confetti as they slowly floated down to the floor. He said nothing. I probably would have killed him if he said anything. Thank goodness he didn't.

I knew that my time was up. It was becoming more difficult to call Jon at free will. It almost seemed that Jon was not interested in playing anymore. I knew that it was time to move forward in my life. I disconnected my pager and cell phone. I stopped using drugs and alcohol and decided it was time for me to quit the sex industry. I decided to move to a new apartment and begin a new chapter in my life.

Chapter Eleven

It was time for my life to change. I remember telling a friend that some people are given blueprints of their lives illustrating how to journey through their existence and some people are given nothing to follow. I was one of the misfortunate individuals that was not given a blueprint or map to aid my journey through life's unexpected obstacles. I started my life at point "A" and zigzagged my way to point "Z" where other people went from point "A" to point "Z" in a single straight line. I needed to let go of my pain, anguish, despair and guilt in order to move forward. I needed to forgive others and myself for who I was as well as what others have done to me. This required letting go of the past and setting goals for my future. The other internal struggle was to "come out" to friends and family.

In order to move forward in the path of emotional growth, I needed to get cleaned-up. It required sobering myself from alcohol, drugs and the sexual addiction. Without the aid of therapists, counselors or support groups, I managed to slowly get better. I began to live my life as a responsible adult for the first time in my life. I stopped drinking and taking drugs and began to minimize my visits to gay bars where the temptations of such substances where present. As I was recovering from the alcohol, drugs and sexual addiction, my friends were no longer interested in my company. Gradually, I began to lose contact with my old friends and began to make new friends. Without the drugs and liquor, my sexual promiscuity became more controllable. I was having sex with individuals that I found attractive not because they were paying me. I must admit there were slip-ups, but I managed to get myself back on track after one or two mishaps. I remember that I was at the Copa nightclub one evening when a man in his mid-thirties approached me. He began to speak to me, but I was not interested in him or his boring conversation. Trying to win me over, he bought me a *Screwdriver*. I began to sip the yellow cocktail and soon afterwards his boring conversation was becoming more interesting. He was short and mousy looking. He had a high-pitched voice and an obnoxious laughter. I certainly did not find him attractive. I think his name was Erick, but I can't be sure. Nonetheless, I'll call him Erick. I couldn't believe that I was actually interchanging in conversation with him. It must have been my second *Screwdriver*, or was I on my fourth drink by now. I can't recall. Regardless, I was feeling good and Erick was becoming more interesting. Finally, he asked me if I would consider going to bed with him. Without much hesitation, I said, "Yes, for $150 bucks." He opened his wallet and handed me five $20 bills. I told him, "I said $150 bucks. This is only $100 bucks." As he opened his billfold, he said, "That's all I have." I folded the five bills and placed them inside my jeans. I asked him to follow me to my apartment where I fucked the shit out of him. This was my last slip-up.

It was a slow and tedious process to let go of the past and of the feelings, which caused me such stagnation. Slowly, I recognized that my life was changing. I was more at peace with myself and had less anger toward my family and friends. I was, without realizing it, letting go of the internal anger and rage that harbored inside me for so many years. For the first time in my life, I was living in the present and not living in the past. Prior to this, my past was dictating my present behaviors and actions. I would react and enact based on my past pains and lack of self-worth. It was no way to continue living. I now had the freedom to live my life without anger, hatred, anguish and guilt. I was obtaining the internal love that allowed me to move forward as a man and a father through the journey of life.

After resolving many of my dysfunctional and unhealthy feelings that encompassed my life, I needed to accomplish one more item. It was probably the most difficult situation that I've had to face, but I knew that I would have to confront the issue to continue to move forward. It was time for me to "come out" to the world. First, I needed to fully accept my homosexuality. I needed to accept the fact that I was gay. Prior to this, I would deny my sexual identity and consider myself a man that liked to have sex with men. I realized that what I wanted in a man had nothing to do with sex, but rather with establishing a deep and emotional love with a man. I had a yearning to be in a loving relationship with a man and not simply have sex with men. It wasn't easy to accept my *gayness,* but I eventually did. I started attending the Metropolitan Community Church where I was accepted as an individual and my sexuality was not an issue. I was part of a religious congregation that accepted me for whom I was and not for whom society wanted me to become. I began to like myself as a complete human being. I learned to love the whole me. Once I fully accepted myself, it was time to spread the news to my family. It wasn't easy, but I knew I needed to "come out." I was afraid and fearful of the rejection from my parents and family. I was afraid to be left alone. I confided my fears to the pastor of the church and I remember him telling me, "You will never be alone. You have God and yourself that loves you." Thanks to those precious words, I have been able to overcome many obstacles in my life. Despite the consequences "coming out" would cause, I decided to tell my family. I needed to live a truthful and honest life, which meant telling my Mom and Dad.

One of the most frightening issues that any gay man faces is "coming out." For many of us "coming out" is a gradual process that takes months or years to complete (or, partially complete). Regardless, it is a very difficult issue; however, for married gay men with children, the issue of "coming out" encompasses a monumental fear. As gay men, we have the fear of family and friends rejecting us, but as married gay men, we have the fear of losing our children. We have all heard horror stories about gay men and women that have lost their parental rights because of their homosexuality. These men and women have been deemed by the judicial courts to be less than appropriate parents in co-raising their children. There have been court judges that have stripped these fathers and mothers from all their parental rights and ordered these gay parents supervised visitations with their children. Sex offenders get better treatment than us. There was a court case not long ago when a father lost all his parental custody to a drug-addicted mother. To make matters worse, not only was the mother a drug addict, but she was also a convicted criminal that served time in prison. What was the judge thinking! I can't blame the fear that many married gay men and women have about "coming out." While society and the judicial system continues to consider us sick, diseased, fornicators, child molesters and a "bad influences" to our children, we will continue to hide in the closet.

I have spoken to several married gay men (and some married gay women) and asked them why they hadn't "come out" to their spouses. The common denominator in their response was "Fear." It is sad that *fear* prevents many people from becoming complete and whole. *Fear* causes men and women to live unhappy lives. *Fear* makes us stay in marriages afraid that we will lose our children. It is *fear* that has led many teenagers to suicide.

Like many married gay man I too had fear. I was afraid of losing custody of my child because of my homosexuality. I was afraid to lose the love that Maybelle once had for me. I was afraid to be abandoned or rejected by my parents. I was afraid of society. I was afraid of the unknown. I was fearful of losing everything I cherished and loved. Despite the consequences, I needed to face my life with honesty and truth regardless of my fears.

The first person I told of the news was my brother and his wife. His wife on several occasions had confronted me about the issue of homosexuality. Over drinks one night, she asked me if I was gay. She had her suspicions, but I simply denied her the truth. My life continued as normal and mundane until one day I visited my brother and his wife with a man I was dating. Peter was probably the most effeminate man they had ever seen. He was very handsome, but too *nelly* to pass as straight. The front door opened and I introduced Peter and his Yorkshire terrier to my brother and his wife. They only took one quick glance and knew he was *queer*. We visited for an hour before heading back to my place. I knew that my brother or sister-in-law would call me to discuss my new friend. They did. That same night my brother called and asked me, "Is Peter your hairdresser?" Actually, Peter was my hair stylist at the time. I giggled at his comment and told him that I needed to have a long talk with him. I drove to my brother's home later that evening.

It wasn't five minutes after I entered their home when my sister-in-law began the questioning. After three or four probing and interrogating questions, I finally told them. "I need to tell you guys something. I'm gay." I told them in a matter of fact type of voice. My brother and Maybelle both looked at me and in unison said, "We still love you." I felt a hundred pounds had been lifted from my shoulders. My brother's main concern was my parents. He didn't want me to tell my parents. He was too afraid of their reaction to the news. Unfortunately, I had lived in a secret for a long time and despite their reaction to the news I would eventually tell my Mom and Dad.

I decided to visit my parents one autumn day in the early evening. As usual, I would frequent their house and have dinner before heading home to my apartment. This particular day I decided to stay a bit longer. It was a cool and breezy evening and I sat outside on the porch. I called my Mom to sit with me and enjoy the evening air. She agreed and came outside to join me. For ten minutes, there was no conversation. Despite the silence, I knew that my Mother was intrigued at my secret lifestyle. I broke the silence by asking her whether she wanted to ask me anything that might concern her about my life. She said, "Yes." She began the questioning. For starters she asked, "Are you into drugs?" Then, "Are you doing something wrong?" She continued to ask me, "Are you living a destructive life?" I answered, "no", "no" and "NO." I then made a comment to her. I said, "If there is something you want to ask me don't be afraid. However, be prepared for an honest response." Then she asked me, "Are you *maricon?*" I replied, "Yes." There was an intense silence and then I said, "I don't expect for you to understand my life nor accept me, but I do demand respect from you. If you can't give me respect, tell me now and I will never step foot into this house again. I love you and I want you to be a part of my life; however, if you can only love me by putting limitations and conditions to your love, I want no part of that love." She got up from her chair and opened her arms to me and without a tear hugged me. She said, "I will love you no matter who or what you are." I was in awe. She did ask me not to tell my Father and I respected her wishes for the time being. Her two main concerns were revealing the secret to my Father and of course, AIDS. I reassured her that I always practiced safe sex and that nothing was going to happen to my health. As for my Father, I was also concerned about how he would react to the news, but my intentions were to tell him regardless.

My relationship with my Mother became better without having the wall of my sexuality dividing us. She gradually began asking me whom I was dating and I would tell her all the details of my dates. I would tell her everything except the *nitty gritty* stuff. My relationship with my Mother had become stronger. We began to speak on a daily basis and reached another level of love. I felt there were no walls between my Mother and I any longer. It was the relationship I always dreamed about. Now, I needed to prepare myself for my Father's reaction to the news. My brother and Mother didn't want me to "come out" to him due to his health. Needless to say, my Father's health was fine. Some people think that as a person ages their health deteriorates. This was the mentality of my Mom and brother. They felt that my Father was old and therefore ill and frail. Actually, he is healthier than me. My intentions were not to make him have a stroke or die of a major heart attack when he heard the news. Instead, I wanted to be honest and truthful about my life. I wanted to know whether he would still love me knowing I was gay. I knew that I needed for him to know regardless.

It was one year or longer from the date I spoke to my Mom and brother before I decided to "come out" to my Dad. In the interim, many arguments between my Mother, brother and myself occurred concerning the topic. Finally, I made the choice to tell him. My Dad is brusque which makes him react to situations abruptly. Due to his personality, I took another approach in delivering the news. I decided to write a long and detailed letter to him. I knew that telling him personally would not be the best approach. He simply would turn around and walk away from me. However, a letter illustrating the love I had for him would make him think twice about his reactions and thought process. I wrote him a seven-page letter.

I began to write a long and detailed letter to my Father. It took seven hand written pages to express the pain that I had lived with for such a long time and the need I had to express my secret life to him. I chose not to write the word "gay" or "homosexual", but with many descriptive adjectives I was able to stress my point across to him. I decided to hand deliver this letter to him one evening and instructed him to open the envelope only after I had left the room. It was the 2nd day of January when I drove to his home and hand-delivered the letter. I handed the tan envelope and gave him instructions when to open the concealed revelation. Within twenty minutes my car phone was ringing. I looked at the incoming call and recognized the seven numbers on the display to be those of my Father's telephone. I picked up the phone and without a greeting heard a load childlike sobbing on the other end of the receiver. It was my Dad. He was incoherent and emotional, but I managed to calm him down. I was able to decipher his words while he sobbed asking me to return to his house. My heart began to beat and pound harder and harder, but I agreed to his request. I turned my car around and began to retrace the road back to my parent's home.

He was waiting for me at the door. I didn't even have to knock or ring the doorbell. He was standing behind the door waiting for me. When he opened the door, I saw a frail and weeping man. A man I have never seen before. A man that was not the powerful and strong man I was familiar with. He held out his arms and embraced me, as he never had done. His dripping tears made my own cheeks wet with the salty fluid as he continued to hold me tightly against his body. He held me for endless minutes whispering, "I love you, I love you, I love you." I managed to guide him to the den where we sat and said nothing for several minutes. Through the whimpering voice and occasional sob that made his sentences broken and difficult to understand, I heard him say, "How could you? How could you?" He would repeat these words over and over again. I then asked him if he was saddened by my news. Surprisingly, he said, "No." Still with reddened and watery eyes, he looked at me and said the most beautiful words I have ever heard him say to me. His comment was, "I am not saddened by who you are, but I am disappointed because you thought I would reject you. I will never reject, abandon or neglect you. You are my son and I love you no matter what or who you are or become. Furthermore, I will accept you and whomever you decide to love in your life. I am your father and it's my responsibility to love and give you support in whatever makes you happy." As he was saying these words to me, my heart was being squeezed tighter and tighter. I was in awe at his love and support. I too began to get watery eyes and soon I broke into a silent whimper as we embraced. I was astonished at his reaction. I finally had the unconditional love I yearned from my Father. My life was coming together. Finally, it was making sense. Or, was it?

Revealing my homosexuality to my parents allowed me to bring my dates to dinner parties and family gatherings. My parents were always accepting of all my boyfriends and never treated anyone with a lack of respect. During this time, I was still in somewhat of a transitional period with Maybelle. In other words, Maybelle was the only person that was not accepting my homosexuality. However, I felt free to live my life and date men. I also enjoyed how I was evolving.

My next hurdle was to enlighten Maybelle about who I was and the love I have towards her. I was afraid of vengeance from her. I was fearful of what she might do to me in respect to my daughter. Revealing the news to my parents had very little consequences; however, "coming out" to Maybelle had more severe ramifications. Despite the consequences and ramifications, I needed to be truthful with everyone regardless of what occurred.

I invited her to dinner one evening where we could discuss the issue at hand. I chose a public establishment just in case she would be tempted to make a scene. I figured that the restaurant patrons might be reason enough for her to act rational. Not surprisingly, she responded just like I had suspected. She became angry with me when I revealed that I had made a choice to continue my life as a gay man. She was hopeful that I would reconsider my choices and return home to her, but she was mistaken. I continued to express my love to Maybelle despite her obvious anger, but she didn't want to hear it. With every minute that lapsed, Maybelle's body became more contorted and tight from her frustration and anger towards me. I noticed the disappointment in her voice as she interrogated me with questions. The veins of her neck were bulging and pulsating as she tried to gather herself with poise. She asked me whether I had cheated on her with a man while married. I answered, "Yes." She pushed her dinner plate away and looked at me with disgust and sickness, as her jugulars were dilated and pulsating in a constant rhythm. She excused herself and walked toward the lady's rest room where she vomited, sobbed or did both. She returned minutes later with swollen lids and eyes from the sadness of the devastating choice I had made. Her entire body was frigid and tight, as her frustration and anger grew more intense. I can still recall her last statement before we left the restaurant. She said to me, "It would have been easier for me to discover your dead body than discovering that you were gay." She much rather me tell her I was bisexual than gay. Bisexuality allowed her hope in my return home whereas being gay gave her no hope what so ever. Needless to say, dinner ended much sooner than expected.

I suppose that it is more difficult for your spouse to accept the issue of homosexuality than friends or family. It is more devastating to the spouse because he/she feels that the marriage was a lie from the beginning. This was the case with Maybelle. She didn't and still hasn't accepted my homosexuality. Her irrational behavior, anger and frustration have been demonstrated in more than one incident towards me. It has been five years and still she has a surmountable amount of pain, anger and grief about the loss of her marriage. I feel that her anger and grief comes from the notion of her thinking that our marriage was a farce. It wasn't, yet the man she loved, trusted and valued shattered her dreams, goals and life. She was severely injured from my "coming out" because it directly affected her as well. It directly affected her dreams of growing old with the man she married.

The truth is that I've always known of my sexual torment. Ever since I was young, I had to deal with the demons of my sexuality, but I was afraid of the consequences that telling my parents would have on me. Hence, I suppressed my sexuality giving me the opportunity to live a life without pain, torment or despair. Surprisingly, even though I suppressed my sexuality for more than two decades, I continued to live in pain, torment and despair throughout my life. My intentions were not to lie and deceive Maybelle when I married her, but to hide the truth from myself. Marriage allowed me protection from my own demons and made me forget my homosexuality. Or, so I thought. I hid myself behind our marriage and I hid my life behind our white picket fence. Nonetheless, I never meant to do any of this intentionally, but it still happened. I still caused her irrepressible pain revealing my own secret. I needed to make her understand that my love for her was true. Despite my intentions, I fell madly in love with her as a person regardless of my homosexuality. However, I never fell in love with her as a wife. It was a love that was deep and true, but never a love that a man should feel for his wife. Today, I realize that my love for Maybelle was similar to feelings I share for my Mother, sister, aunt, etc. It was a love that was more platonic than sexual. It was a companionship love. My life with Maybelle would have been perfect if the marriage was sexless. It would have been the ideal relationship if only I didn't have to have sex with her. Unfortunately, sex is not only important, but also integral in any relationship. I loved to spend time with her and plan our future together. I just hated to have sex with her. I was having sex to relieve myself, but not because I wanted to make love to her. I have never made love to a woman. I have fucked plenty of women, but never made love.

Maybelle always asked me that it seemed that I never connected with her sexually. She was correct. Maybelle one day said to me, "It seems that you separate sex from love." I couldn't understand that statement until recently. When we were sexually intimate, I was not making love, but simply having sex. Sexual intimacy was a mechanical or robotic activity rather than an emotional bonding. However, with a man, the connection between love and sex co-exists together.

I have never felt about anyone as I did (and still do) about Maybelle. I would look forward to spending time with her. Our conversations and our time together were well appreciated. We would walk holding our hands tightly and hold each other to sleep every night. On weekends, we would always go to dinner, movies, theaters or simply stay home relaxing. Spending time with Maybelle was the highlight of my weekends. I loved to cuddle and take long walks with her. I enjoyed the conversations we shared. I admired her beauty and elegance when she dressed in a cocktail dress. I enjoyed her companionship at the opera and theater. However, the enjoyment would end when it was time to return home. She wanted to make the evening complete by making love. I wanted to undress and go to bed. Seductively, she would remove her cocktail dress revealing a sexy lingerie. Any man would kill to have what I had. I simply would look at her body without excitement. I would express my exhaustion and quickly go into a deep sleep. My rejection toward her was constant. I hated myself for putting her through such emotional abuse.

After our sixth year of marriage, our sexual intimacy was decreasing quickly. Sexual intercourse was becoming a mechanical procedure rather than an interpersonal exchange of emotions. It was fucking. However, she was still the most important part of my life. I still loved holding her hand on our long walks and cuddling up beside her to sleep. I enjoyed her as a friend, companion, and partner, but I never admired her as a wife. As my homosexuality began to surface, I gradually stopped caressing her body and then I stopped kissing her. We seldom had sex. I felt impotent knowing I couldn't fulfill her needs by simply giving her a kiss or passionately caressing her body. Our sexual intimacy went from several times per week to once or twice a month. We knew we had a problem, but it was not spoken about. It was taboo to speak about what was going on in our relationship. I believe that Maybelle was afraid to open the can of worms if the topic about sex was brought into light. So, we continued to live in silence ignoring our sexual problems. Our sexless marriage continued for the next five years. The gradual disappearance of our sexual intimacy didn't happen overnight, but over a period of years. However, when it was gone, it was gone forever. It is sad to write these words, as I remember her yearning for a kiss or a touch. I am saddened that a kiss or a soft touch to her body would have demonstrated my love and devotion to the person I loved more than anyone else in my life. If only I would have kissed her or touched her body, I could have (would have) saved my marriage. I couldn't. Some other force inside my body was pulling me in another direction.

When I finally made the decision to leave my home and family, I told Maybelle that I needed some time to sort things out in my head. It was the time I needed to continue hiding my secret. I needed time to prevent her suspicion about my *queerness*. I had to tell her the truth, but it was *fear* that kept my secrets hidden inside the closet. I didn't have to tell her. She discovered my secret herself. How sad.

Chapter Twelve

I've had several hundred sexual encounters, several dozen dates and three significant boyfriends that have impacted my life. Estefan was ten years my senior. He was a handsome Italian man that possessed everything I've ever wanted in a man. His dark hair was speckled with gray accenting his light green eyes. His chest, stomach and legs were a thick coat of dark black fur that made me melt in excitement every time I would look at his naked body. Estefan had a nine-year-old daughter and was divorced from his wife when I met him. He was caring and understanding especially about Maybelle's irrational behavior. He was almost perfect. The one thing he lacked was intelligent conversation. He wasn't the smartest man on the universe and therefore his conversations lacked substance, but I fell in love anyway. Much to my chagrin, so did Maybelle. It was an ironic occurrence, but Estefan and Maybelle became close friends. Actually, they were more than just close friends.

Maybelle was never joyous when I fell in love with a man. She would be fine as long as I dated and my emotions were not involved deeply with another man. However, when she suspected that my affection was increasing toward someone else she would do anything to sabotage the relationship. I suppose she felt abandoned and unloved when my energies were spent on another person other than her. Regardless of her reasoning, it was very difficult to deal with her irrational and crazy behavior.

I remember one such evening. Estefan and I were making love in my apartment when we heard someone knocking at the front door. It was past midnight and we were both curious to see who the late night visitor might have been. I walked to the door and looked through the peephole and saw Maybelle's frazzled face on the other side of the wooden door. I asked her what she needed and she told me to open the door. I refused and told her

I had company and could not have a conversation with her at that time. Her composure was immediately lost. She began to kick and bang on the apartment door. Estefan and I were both in the bedroom wondering what to do. I was afraid to let her in and terrified of her irrational behavior. From my bedroom window, I would see her running up and down the stairs yelling and screaming obscenities at me. "YOU FUCKIN' *FAG-GOT*, OPEN THE FUCKIN' DOOR," she yelled. I went to the balcony where I was able to see her Mercedes Benz double-parked and Alexa Rae strapped inside her car seat. She saw me on the balcony and began to demand to let her inside the apartment. Again, I refused. I was frightened at her irrational behavior. She ran to her car and opened the trunk where several cardboard boxes filled with items were located. She began to grab items from the boxes and throw them up to the balcony. When I saw the first flying object come towards me, I dodged and headed inside. I heard shattering glass, as the items would hit the concrete balcony. I reached for the phone and called the police. Several minutes later, two police cars arrived and Maybelle began to run back to her car. The uniformed men pulled her from the inside of her car and pushed her against the driver's side of the white Mercedes Benz. One of the police officers had his hand on her head pressing her cheeks against the white metal of her car. The other was putting handcuffs on her. I went downstairs to speak to the police officers pleading not to press charges. As they were interrogating me, I was holding Alexa Rae trying to soothe her crying caused by the blue strobe lights and loud sirens. As I was speaking to the officers, my eyes wondered toward Maybelle and saw her eyes filled with pain and hurt. I saw as they escorted her handcuffed body into one of the police cars. I couldn't hold it in any longer and began to cry. I pleaded with the two officers to let her go and luckily they were persuaded not to press charges. I was asked to stay with Alexa Rae and she was ordered to drive home. As I was walking toward my apartment, I saw shattered glass and pieces of documents lying on the pavement. The flying objects were my framed college degrees and professional awards. I began to gather as many of the documents as possible and then went upstairs to put Alexa Rae to sleep. The entire evening I saw the blue lights and heard the loud sirens in my dreams. What a horrifying experience.

Maybelle never forgave me for calling the cops on her, but eventually she forgot. She continued to be a nuisance in my relationship with Estefan, but she knew where to draw the line. Several months after the police incident, Maybelle began to insist on meeting Estefan. Her rationale was that Alexa Rae was spending too much time over my apartment with Estefan and I. It seemed to me that she was more curious about whom he was then whether he was a pedophile. Despite her ulterior motives, it seemed logical for her to meet the man I was sharing my life. I spoke to Estefan and we agreed to a mutual meeting. I invited both of them to dinner where Maybelle had the opportunity to introduce herself and ask as many questions as she deemed necessary. I arrived at the restaurant first and Maybelle followed several minutes later. Last to arrive was Estefan. I waved from our table trying to get his attention. He approached us and introduced himself to Maybelle. We had a pleasant dinner with lots of conversation, questions and even some laughter. I suspected the laughter was from the excessive alcoholic beverages that Estefan and Maybelle were consuming. The drinking continued until I noticed that both of them were moderately *buzzed*. I offered to drive Maybelle's car home, but she insisted that it was still early and she would like to go dancing at a gay club. Yes, a gay club. I looked at Estefan and nodded in disapproval at Maybelle's recommendation. However, the evening was going well and I thought to myself, *Why end it now?* Hence, with little persuasion, I agreed to Maybelle's suggestion. We left two vehicles at the restaurant parking lot and all three of us drove in Estefan's car to Electra.

We arrived at the dance club shortly after leaving the restaurant. Maybelle and Estefan were hitting it off nicely. They continued to drink alcohol and I watched their new friendship evolve from the bar counter and into the dance floor. I decided to buy myself a shot of *Kamikaze* while I stood watching Maybelle's seductive dance moves with my boyfriend.

One shot of the powerful liquid wasn't enough to anesthetize my mind as I watched my boyfriend and Maybelle dance together, so I ordered a second shot. Soon afterwards, a third shot of the thick clear liquid was swallowed. The scene became less frightening and more enticing after the consumption of the alcoholic liquid. I managed to make my way into the dance floor where I joined Estefan and Maybelle. Alcohol makes you do some weird things. It wasn't long after I joined the dance dual when my tongue was inside Maybelle's mouth and Estefan was grabbing Maybelle's tits. The sexual groping and touching continued until we were horny for each other's body. We continued to dance well into the night until the dark dance floor lit up with bright lights telling its patrons it was time to go home. We walked to Estefan's car where neither one of us were functional to drive, but we did. Maybelle sat in the back seat while Estefan sat on the front passenger seat and I drove the white sporty Volkswagen Jetta back to my apartment. We arrived late and I offered Maybelle to sleep over taking into consideration her condition. She agreed. We sat around the floor and continued to drink alcohol. I dimmed the lights and lit several candles around the apartment giving a romantic glow to the scene. Estefan rolled a joint. Combining the effect of the pot with the alcohol gave us permission to get more sexual. We began to grope each other's body and soon we were naked on the floor. I guided Maybelle and Estefan into the bedroom where we continued the three-way adventure.

I was licking Maybelle's cunt while Estefan was eating my asshole. I was certainly the ringleader of the *manage au tois* and would position the two of them as I felt necessary. We did oral suck circles and all sorts of different sexual positions. However, the position that made me almost blow my load was when I had Maybelle on her back and I told Estefan to fuck her. He was positioned over her while he pounded his dick inside her wet pussy. His legs wide open over her body gave me easy access to his own hairy hole. I then came from behind and lubed his ass with spit and began to fuck him. The deeper I pushed inside him the deeper he penetrated Maybelle and the more they both moaned. Then we switched. I began to fuck Maybelle while Estefan's hands opened my ass cheeks and tongued my ass and balls. I sat Maybelle on top of me and she began to ride my cock while Estefan continued the licking. As Maybelle lifted her body upward, Estefan would grab hold of my dick and then reinsert it into her wet pussy. I positioned her below me again and began to fuck her hard. I spread her legs wide allowing me deeper entry into her cunt and from behind I felt Stephen's mouth suck my pussy-juiced dick. It was the most incredible sex I've ever had. After several hours, we finally began to reach orgasm. Maybelle was first, than Estefan, then Maybelle again and then me. For the *grand finale,* Estefan and I went down on Maybelle's pussy assisting her as she reached her third orgasm. Needless to say, we slept very well that night.

Estefan, Maybelle and I continued our relationship. On Mondays and Wednesdays, Estefan would spend the evenings with me and on Tuesdays and Thursdays he would spend the nights with Maybelle. Fridays through Sundays we would share each other in bed. It seemed that the only person that was not satisfied with the arrangement was me. I didn't want to share my boyfriend and least of all with Maybelle. However, I loved him and didn't want to lose him, so I continued the weird and peculiar relationship. I feel that Maybelle chose to continue the *manage au tois* only because she didn't want to lose me either. Her participation in the threesome allowed her to have me part-time to herself. I know she rather have not shared me, but she rather have shared me with another man than to lose me altogether.

Maybelle didn't respect the nights that Estefan and I would spend together. On Mondays and Wednesdays, she would constantly telephone and make unexpected visits to the apartment. It was obvious that she was jealous. After several weeks of our weird relationship, I noticed that Maybelle's jealousy was getting out of control. She made it clear to us that she didn't want Estefan and I to have private days together. She rather Estefan and I spend every night with her. Unfortunately, I didn't want this. I needed to feel the body of a man all to myself and I began to resent our modern and alternate relationship. Five or six months into our bizarre relationship, I decided to have a talk with Maybelle and Estefan.

We met one evening at my apartment where I began to express my concerns and disappointments in the relationship. After an hour or two of talking and discussing my concerns, I decided that I needed to call it quits. I basically told Estefan and Maybelle that the stress involved in our relationship was too much for me to handle and therefore wanted no part in the continuance of the threesome. Honestly, I felt Estefan was going home with me that night. Much to my surprise, Estefan chose to sleep with Maybelle that evening. Needless to say, I ended my relationship with Estefan that night. However, Maybelle and Estefan continued their relationship for several months afterwards until she realized that he was *queerer* than me. Estefan and I have never spoken again.

It didn't take me long to start where I had left off. The day after I broke-up with Estefan I was at the bars. I met Charles. Then Rick, Orlando, Jeff, Randy, David, Dominique, Eddie, Todd, Bill, Darrel, and many, many others. I also enjoyed several three-ways and four-ways and took home several dozen *tricks*. As a matter of fact, in 1998, I counted 108 men with whom I had exchanged sexual pleasures. I have always been obsessed with writing everyone I went to bed with on a piece of paper. I have never understood this sick obsession, but it allowed me to keep track of my most precious sexual encounters. I wasn't hustling men, but simply having a good time fucking them. However, the months past and soon I began to get tired of fucking around and decided that it was time for a steady boyfriend. I was in search of a new steady man in my life. Several months after ending my relationship with Estefan, I was introduced to Maurice.

He was a short, hairy, dark haired farm boy from Upstate New York. I met him on a Sunday evening while I was on a disastrous blind date with someone else. I believe the troll's name was Joe. Anyway, I spoke to Maurice that night for approximately ten minutes. Ten minutes was enough to make me want to pursue him further. Unfortunately, Maurice lived in California. I couldn't keep my mind off him. I didn't know how to reach him in California. The night we met we didn't speak much and neither one of us gave a "sign" of our mutual attraction. Nonetheless, I was certainly attracted to him. The following Sunday I woke up with the determination to call him in California. I called several of my friends, but no one knew Maurice's telephone number. I had reached a dead end. My last alternative was to call the Los Angeles information telephone directory and try to obtain his telephone through that avenue. Hopefully, his number would be listed. Unfortunately, his telephone was a non-published number. I was very disappointed at the second dead end; however, I called the California operator a second time and explained that I was trying to reach Maurice from Florida to deliver a notice of death in his family. Without much delay, the operator connected my call directly to his home. After several rings, the answering machine picked-up with his recorded voice instructing the caller to leave a message. I hesitated for several seconds, but hung up the receiver without leaving a message. Several hours later, I called the Los Angeles operator a third time where she connected my call directly to his home, but only after telling her the same lie. Once again, the operator was receptive and connected my call to Maurice's home.

The phone rang three or four times before a voice answered with a simple, "Hello." He was putting groceries away when he received my unexpected phone call. "Hello, Maurice?" I said. He recognized my voice instantaneously and told me he was shocked to hear my voice. The first several minutes of our conversation were awkward, but then our words seemed to flow easily. We spoke three hours that night and everyday thereafter until I decided to pay him a visit two months later.

Every day for two months I spoke to Maurice on the telephone. My long distance telephone charges were almost a mortgage payment, but it was worth every penny. Because of the different time zones, I usually would be asleep when he would call me. However, waking-up to his voice was pleasurable. Despite my drowsiness, we still managed to speak for hours on end. Considering the fact that we only met for ten minutes and didn't know too much about each other, we soon felt a bond and connection. I felt comfortable with Maurice because he was easy to speak with and he was a good listener as well. Days followed and our telephone courtship continued to evolve. As the weeks continued to pass, my feelings for Maurice grew stronger. I began to refer to him as my "boyfriend" to my friends. My close friends thought I was crazy. I must point out, I thought I was crazy too. It was invigorating to have such strong feelings toward a man that I had never kissed nor made love with before. It was mind twisting and boggling, but I simply accepted the fact that I was falling in love with a man I didn't know much about.

As the weeks continued, I began to forget what Maurice looked like physically. I didn't know whether he was balding or had a full head of hair, whether he was smooth or hairy, short or tall, fat or thin. I had forgotten everything about him. I had even forgotten his eye color. Maurice asked me one evening to tell him what color eyes he had. I guessed twice and was wrong on both accounts. His eyes were crystalline blue and I guessed brown and green. He giggled at the notion that I couldn't remember anything about him and I challenged him to describe me. He recalled everything about me perfectly. At this stage in the telephonic relationship, it made no difference what he looked like. I truly cared for him despite his physical appearance. The impact he made in my life was monumental. He was the first man that I grew to have such strong feelings and emotions toward without having sex. The more I spoke to him the stronger my feelings became. I remember yearning for him several nights and masturbating to his phantom image inside my mind. As our comfort level grew with each other, we began to feel at ease sharing the pleasures of phone sex. It was the next best thing to having him next to me. I never asked him whether he was a *bottom* or a *top*, but through our erotic conversations it was obvious he was a *bottom*. Despite our lack of physical contact and intimacy, we had awesome telephonic sex. I couldn't wait to get my hands on his body. I wanted to kiss his lips and feel his body next to mine. We continued to have our daily rapport and within one month from our initial meeting he expressed his devotional feelings towards me. It occurred one evening as we were saying good night. After his traditional, "Good night and sweet dreams," he said, "I love you." I was in shock. I didn't know what to say or do when I heard him say those three words. I was mesmerized and simply said, "Thank you."

I was dumbfounded at the idea that Maurice loved me. I couldn't understand how anyone could feel such strong feelings without actually knowing the person they supposedly loved. Our conversation would never end without him expressing his love towards me. I tried never to respond, but only thanked him for his sweet words of affections. However, one evening as he began to express his love and devotion towards me, I asked him if he had ever loved anyone as he loved me. He replied, "No." I went on to say, "How can you love me? You don't know me. You simply know the person you hear over the telephone and the person that I have described to be me." He simply said, "Alex, I know that I love you." I was simply trying to illustrate to Maurice that he was to embark in a relationship with a man that had many skeletons hidden away in a closet. Specifically, it was a skeleton of an ex-whore that I was hiding. After several weeks, I managed to tell him the truth about myself. I told him everything from my sexual addiction to my sex-for-pay career. I even told him about my drug and alcohol abuse. I suppose that my fear was that I was going to fall in love with Maurice and after he found out the truth he would break-up with me. After telling him about all my skeletons, he simply told me that my past didn't scare him. He reassured me by saying, "I trust you and have faith in you." Our courtship continued. I made plans to visit Los Angeles two months after the day we met.

We were both ecstatic anticipating the day we would eventually meet in person. We would count the days remaining for my trip as prisoners count days for parole behind prison walls. I couldn't believe we would actually meet in person. The days drew nearer and nearer as we continued our daily conversations.

The trip from Florida to California is very tiresome and boring. I remember I read several chapters of a novel and watched *Working 9 to 5* costarring Dolly Parton. Finally, the flight attendants gave me some breakfast and I napped for an hour or so. Upon waking from my nap, I wrote an entry in my traveling journal. Finally, I heard the pilot make the announcement that we would be landing shortly. I finished writing my final thoughts in my journal and began to organize my belongings. It was time to land the plane in Los Angeles. It was a DC 10 and inside the large metal bird was approximately three hundred passengers. I was one of the last passengers to disembark the aircraft. As I walked out of the airplane, I came to the terminal gate where hundreds of people awaited their family and friends. I had previously described to Maurice what I was wearing and he told me his outfit. This allowed us to identify each other easily through the herd of people standing around the terminal gate. It was easy to identify me because I was wearing leather-braided suspenders. I walked slowly allowing Maurice to pick me out from the mass of people. I glanced around looking for someone short, hairy, with a goatee and wearing blue jeans and a yellow Tommy Hilfilger shirt. There was no one that fit his description. I began to feel let down and abandoned. I sat for a short moment and than decided to walk toward the baggage claim area. Several hundred yards walking toward me was a man wearing a yellow shirt and blue jeans. I was unable to see the Tommy Hilfiger logo, but there was a possibility it was Maurice. As the distance began to decrease between us, I was able to notice he had a goatee. The distance got shorter and I noticed he was a shorter man than myself. We continued toward each other and I was able to discern the dark chest hair behind the yellow shirt. Finally, I was able to see what appeared to be the Tommy Hilfiger logo on his shirt. It was he. It was actually Maurice. He was much more handsome than I had imagined. He was truly beautiful. I gave him a half smile and he returned it with a beautiful smile of his own. When we got face-to-face, I held him in my arms and gave him a kiss on the lips. However, not much conversation was exchanged. At first, it was as if two friends had met. He asked me the usual questions, "How was your trip? Tired? Hungry?" and so on. We were nervous, shocked and shy. We spoke in short sentences. I thought that initially he was not interested in me, but that was not the case. We just felt weird. It definitely felt strange meeting the person you love for the first time. We got my luggage and headed out toward the parking garage.

My five-day stay in Los Angeles was interesting. Yes, interesting for a lack of a better word. I didn't know how to make sense of my feelings towards him. I didn't know what to say or how to hold him, touch him or even make love to him. The first days visiting Maurice was awkward, but by the end of my five-day stay, I was getting use to my new boyfriend. I wish I could have stayed longer, but I needed to get back to my office in Miami. My five-days with Maurice were interesting, but enjoyable. I enjoyed every moment and treasured every memory spent with him. I remember one day we drove the hillsides along the pacific ocean when we decided to park his white Dodge Ram pickup and walk down to the shore. The shoreline was filled with colorful smooth stones. Holding each other's hands as we walked barefoot along the breaking waves, we gathered several containers of the colorful rocks. Before we knew it, we had gathered several dozens of the colorful stones. I remember this day with such fond memories. I managed to bring the stones to Miami where I carefully placed them in a cylindrical glass vase and tied a raffia bow around the neck of the glass container. I placed the heavy vase on my night table as a constant reminder of our relationship.

Our relationship continued to grow and strengthen while we were two thousand miles away. His job contract ended in mid March and he decided not to renew his contract for the following year. On March 15, Maurice gave me the news he was moving to Miami. I was elated. On March 18, I drove to Miami International Airport awaiting his arrival.

He moved in with me upon his arrival from California. He was the male partner I always wanted. A man that I would love, share my life, goals and dreams. We began to reorganize closet space and drawer space to make room for my new live-in boyfriend. We redecorated my home to accommodate his taste and within a week we were both situated into our new love nest. However, with my new roommate arrived new problems.

As soon as Maybelle became aware of the new person in my life her behavior began to change. Maybelle became irrational once again. Her anger and irrational behavior were less in magnitude than when I was dating Estefan, but it was still difficult to deal with her at times. It was impossible for her to see me happy and in love with a man.

One early morning, Maurice and I woke up to notice Maybelle's car parked on our driveway. I wondered what she was doing there early in the morning and opened the door to meet her outside. She was bent over the steering wheel fast asleep. I gently tapped the window of her car and she woke up startled. She opened the door and asked me to please let her in the house. We sat in the living room sofa where she began to cry and begged me to come home to her. Her irrational behavior continued until it was replaced with anger and then rage. Maurice was in the bedroom and Maybelle and I were in the living room. Her yelling continued to fill the entire house and I simply asked her to leave. She refused. Her rage continued and began to throw anything she could find at me. Glass ashtrays and small porcelain figurines made shattering music as they smashed against the walls. Yet, Maurice never left the bedroom. As she continued her frenzy, I decided to call the police once again. The phone call scared her sufficiently that she decided to leave the house, but only after throwing the umbrella stand at me. The police officers arrived moments later to a much more quiet home where I decided not to press charges on the mother of my child.

She was mad. She would call our home at all times of the night and hang up when we picked up the receiver. She would visit our home while Maurice and I were having dinner and begin to scream obscenities and insults from the yard. It was obvious she was in pain and hurting deeply. It was emotionally difficult for me to see Maybelle in such disarray. It hurt me to see the woman I loved become so mentally disturbed. Above all, it was Maurice that was put in the middle of this madness. In all honesty, he should not have put up with any of it. He never said anything. He would simply ignore the incident(s) and continued his normal routine. However, inside he was brewing a pot of anger and resentment. The phone calls, the visits, the yells and screams would all affect me. I allowed them to affect me. As I would watch Maybelle running around the yard screaming and calling me names, I would only feel my own pain as the causative agent of her behavior. My guilt and pain were drowning me from the inside out, but I did nothing except gasp for air trying to keep myself afloat.

I recall one specific night that Maurice arrived early from work and decided to prepare dinner for us. I arrived home to see our small dining room table beautifully decorated and the odor of a delectable dinner waiting for me. Two candles were lit creating a shimmering romance in the air. He wasn't much of a cook, but tonight he was Betty Crocker. He prepared everything perfectly and beautifully. He poked his body out of the kitchen to greet me wearing nothing except a black thong underwear. He looked scrumptious. He loosened my tie, unbuttoned my shirt and helped me get out of my dress slacks. He then began to slowly pull down my underwear revealing my hard dick. Naked and with a stiff dick, I sat down at the dining room table for what appeared to be a most delightful evening with my lover. As I savored the fish he baked, I began to get sadder and sadder until finally I began to cry. Then, it became an uncontrollable sob. He couldn't understand my sadness, but I was well aware of my pain. The pain I felt that night was because of my own happiness. I was saddened that I was so happy and Maybelle was miserable. My love for Maybelle was so addictive that I didn't allow myself happiness with anyone including Maurice.

The weeks continued to move forward in our lives, but Maurice was losing interest. I never blamed him. I allowed my guilt and sorrow to govern my relationship. Of course, Maurice had many issues that I still haven't figured out. Nonetheless, he simply got fed up with my shit. Despite our endless attempts, Maurice one afternoon expressed his unhappiness with our relationship and decided it was time to move out. I will never forget his piercing words to me, "I just don't love you enough. I've lost hope." Again he said, "I just don't love you enough." I was devastated. I have never felt so lost and empty before. I fell in love with Maurice and I didn't want to lose him, but his mind was made up.

It was late June when he decided to leave. I watched him from our bedroom window leave our home. He gathered a small overnight bag and within minutes was jumping inside his truck. I felt that the entire house was caving in on me. For weeks, I cried and wrote unsent letters to him. For months, I yearned his warmth and touch. Every day of the week, I would think about him. I would think about my love for him. I couldn't manage to get him out of my heart. I told myself that in order for me to move forward I needed to forget Maurice, but more importantly not have my own guilt and torment about leaving Maybelle affect my life. Easier said than done. However, It became simple to forget him when I remembered those piercing words told to me months before, "I just don't love you enough." Every time that a memory would come into my mind, I would think of those words and my love soon became hate. I allowed myself to let go of the love I had for Maurice and began to despise him for saying those words to me. Finally, I realized that Maurice never loved me at all and I would have to let him go. More importantly, I needed to let go of Maybelle in order for me to move forward in life.

I didn't go out for several weeks post my breakup. I would work, go home, eat and sleep. The next day continued the same cycle. The cycle continued week after week after week. Anywhere I would be, I would check my voice messages hoping Maurice had called. He never did. I guess he "never loved me enough." I was left alone again. I needed to start going out and make new friends. Several weeks went by and I began to date again. It seemed awkward at first to kiss someone other than Maurice's lips, but then it became second nature. Within two months, I was back in the swing of things. I was making new friends and becoming reacquainted with old ones. I was dating three or four times a week and *partying* the rest of the week. I was also juggling my daughter between my social life and career. Slowly, Maurice was seeping out of my heart. Slowly. It took one whole year to get him out of my heart. Presently, I still have moments that I can still taste the love I had for him. I have moments that I look back and cherish our fond memories together. I always wonder how it would have been with Maurice. I truly loved him from the bottom of my heart.

I met Johns, and Harrys, Bills and Larrys, but no one came close to Maurice. I was dating everyone that would ask me, but no one was ever good enough. I would compare everyone to Maurice as I compared Maurice to Maybelle. Eventually, I knew that someone would come into my life that would make my heart warm again. However, the wait would be long.

The year of *singlehood* was spent growing emotionally. I needed to deal with many of my own issues, particularly the issue of Maybelle. I allowed myself to make sense of my world. I created solutions to my own problems and moved forward in my own life. I needed to first simplify my life before taking charge of my emotions and feelings. I needed to look at my life not globally, but more detailed specific. I needed to relieve my stress level, enjoy my career and make new friends. I needed to set boundaries with Maybelle and allow myself to love ME. I needed to live for the first time in my life happily. I thought, *How the hell would I ever accomplish all this?* I needed a plan or map to take me where I wanted to be.

The first step was to move closer to my office in Miami. I was commuting three hours a day and concluded that by moving close to my office I would alleviate a substantial amount of stress in my life. I decided to rent my home in Fort Lauderdale and look for an apartment or condominium in Miami. A friend of mine, Marcela, helped me search for a new place. My decision was made on a small condo several blocks from my office. I refurbished the small condominium and finally moved in. When all the final touches were complete, the apartment turned out beautiful. It was several blocks from the office, which saved me a three-hour commute and allowed me to come home for lunch and take a short nap in the afternoons. I started arriving earlier at work and less tired in the morning. I also had more time to go to the gym in the afternoons and spend more time relaxing rather than driving. The condominium was far from my daughter's home, but I was only seeing her on the weekends anyway.

Marcela and I became very close friends. She is what I call a confidant. She has demonstrated a true friendship and I to her. She has been there for me through various stages in my life and has always been nonjudgmental and encouraging. Marcela and I began to spend lots of time together and soon we were making new friends in the bars. It didn't take long for me to adjust to Miami. I also realized that the little hope I had of ever returning with Maurice was now over considering our demographic distance. He was not aware of my move and therefore I felt it would be difficult for him to locate me. Not that he ever would or did.

During this time, I wrote several letters to Maybelle and had several phone conversations with her. I was honest about my feelings and tried to set boundaries with her. I would not allow her sadness, depression or irrational behavior to alter my thinking or behavior. I allowed myself to love her freely without guilt or self-condemnation. I was hopeful that she would do the same, but Maybelle never has developed that skill. She is still in pain from losing her husband, dreams and life.

During my transitional period between Maurice and my next lover, I dated several men. Most men were sexual toys I used for my own sexual gratification. There were several men that I developed an emotional bond, but I knew they were not whom I wanted to share my life. I was patient and careful and didn't want to settle for anyone. This time I wanted my relationship to last.

Two years later after my breakup with Maurice, On November 4, 1999, I met a man that made my heart beat with excitement once again. A man that made Maybelle and all the pains I had inside me disappear. We met at Splash. He was dark and was dressed preppy. I remember as I was leaving the bar I got a glimpse of him standing alongside a wall. I had my keys in my hand, but quickly placed them back into my pocket. I didn't want him to escape. I turned around and headed back to the area he was standing.

He stood against the wall stoic and unapproachable. I began to stare until he finally returned the look. I am rather shy and never approach anyone. However, my friend, Eduardo, was with me that evening and he played cupid. He introduced himself to Victor and later called me over and introduced me. Victor and I hit it off nicely. He had many qualities I was searching for in a man. For starters, he spoke English. It was difficult to find someone that spoke English in Miami, but he did. He was well educated and had a full head of hair. I don't like bald men. It appeared that he was hairy as well. These were all simple and superficial qualities, but that is what I looked for in a man. At least, initially. Physical attraction is of utmost importance to me. I soon realized that he seemed to be emotionally stable. We walked to the bar counter and he ordered me a bottled water where we continued to talk up a storm. We spoke about several topics that ran the gamut from politics to family issues. He didn't seem too keen about my daughter, but every time I mention my daughter to a gay man they seem to jump off their seat (or in this case, off their bar stool). His facial expression changed when I mentioned Alexa Rae. He was shocked. I suppose he was shocked that a gay man fathered a child. Nonetheless, it was obvious that the news of my daughter surprised him. Victor is young. He is seven years my junior, but looks older. Actually, he looks my age. He is a registered nurse at a nearby hospital for the critical care unit. I must admit it had been a long time since my feelings were stirred by anyone. Victor managed to stir my feelings that evening.

He walked me to my car where I wrote my telephone number on a small piece of paper. I didn't ask for his telephone number on purpose. This put the ball in his court. We met on Thursday and I anxiously waited for his call on Friday. To no avail, Victor never called. This caused me great disappointment. I gathered he was just another asshole, so I decided to go out Friday night with a man that I was using as a fuck buddy. His name was Chad. Chad and I would meet occasionally for sex and nothing else. I called him late on Friday evening and told him I was horny and needed to get laid. He graciously agreed and invited me to dinner. After dinner, we headed back to my apartment where we had awesome sex. He is a very handsome man in his early thirties with a very furry body and ass. He worked as a driver for large eighteen-wheeler diesel trucks and was also a diesel engine mechanic. Chad was the epitome of butch. Much to my surprise, he opened his legs quite readily every time I needed a hairy ass. His masculine hairy body moved with synchronized movements as I pounded his furry boy pussy. I would love to see his flaccid dick as I pounded him for endless minutes. One thing that turned me on about Chad was when he would shoot his load. His dick never would get hard. While fucking him, I would see his flaccid penis ooze jism. Slow oozing white *cum* would trickle from his soft dick without him touching it. Then, he would begin to moan loader and short squirts of man juice would escape his piss hole. He was a true *bottom* in every sense of the word. Despite our sexual adventures, we had nothing in common.

I went to work early Saturday morning and upon my return home there was still no messages on my voice mail from Victor. The afternoon was beautifully sunny. It was an excellent day for sunbathing at the gay nudist beach. I arrived at the beach early in the afternoon and didn't take me long before I met a very handsome gay couple. They were laying several feet away from my blanket when I noticed that they were *cruising* me. I went to take a dip in the warm water of the Atlantic and soon they followed. John and Jeff were both very cute. John had a dark complexion with dark hair and blue eyes. He shaved his chest, but a dark shadow of stubble was easily discernible from his neck to his lower stomach. Jeff was smooth and very muscularly toned. He was tan with light brown hair and green eyes. They were both gorgeous. It wasn't long before we were engaged in conversation and from that point on I realized they wanted me. We stepped out of the ocean and dried our bodies and they invited me to lie on their blanket. I took up their offer and gathered my beach gear and went to join them. We all massaged the coconut oil on our bodies and continued to sunbath. After an hour, I asked John and Jeff if they wanted to drive to my apartment where we can get to know each other more privately. Anyhow, the afternoon sun was disappearing into the horizon and we were getting hornier by the minute. We arrived at my place an hour or so afterwards where I suggested a three-person warm shower. We got out of our bathing suits and began to fondle each other before our shower. Needless to say, we had a wonderful time in and out of the shower. Everyone got fucked that Saturday afternoon. After sex, we made plans to have an early dinner in South Beach. After our early meal, I went to John and Jeff's apartment where we had more man sex.

I arrived home Saturday night and checked my voice messages. Victor hadn't called. I was tired from work, the beach and the sex with John and Jeff, but I decided to go out dancing nonetheless. I took a short *disco nap* and by midnight was ready for some more action. I went dancing, but didn't meet anyone that interested me. On my way home Sunday morning, I decided to stop by the bathhouse and pay them a visit.

I arrived at the bathhouse around 4:00 AM discovering the inside busy with horny men. But then again, the bathhouse is busy no matter what time of day you visit. If you are familiar with the Baths, it doesn't take long before you find anxious men ready to give blowjobs or get fucked. Well, within an hour, I received three blowjobs and had fucked a guy that I didn't know his name. He was young, smooth and svelte. I wasn't attracted to him, but when you visit the Baths it is not about finding someone attractive. It's about finding someone to fuck. He must have been in his late teens, but had the tightest ass my dick has ever felt. After *cumming*, I decided it was time for me to leave the disgusting sex building and head home for some much needed sleep.

I slept well into the afternoon on Sunday. My sleep was interrupted by the ringing of the telephone. I clumsily picked up the receiver hoping that it was Victor. It was Chad. We spoke for several minutes and then asked if he could visit me later in the evening. What he meant was he was horny and needed to get fucked. I agreed to his visit and several hours later I was pounding his hole again. The phone began to ring while in bed with Chad, but this time it was Victor. I was still in bed with Chad when I picked up the phone with my slippery lubed hands. "Hello," he said, "May I speak with Alexis?" "Speaking," I said. "It's Victor. I met you last Thursday at Splash. Remember?" Meanwhile, Chad removed my condom and began to suck me until I shot my load in his mouth. "Yes, yes," I replied while my body squirmed from the intensity of my ejaculation.

Chad figured out that I was no longer interested in his company and began wiping his asshole from the thick layer of lubrication. He dressed and gave me a good-bye kiss while I was still on the telephone with Victor. Victor and I spoke for nearly an hour and decided to meet on Monday evening for our first date. I wanted to take him out somewhere special and different, so I decided on a nice stroll in a beautiful golf course in the city of Coral Gables.

I arrived at Victor's apartment complex about 6:30 PM. He had instructed me to wait for him downstairs in my car. I found this odd, but agreed to his request. As I saw him descending the staircase, I got out of my car and went to the passenger's side of the vehicle and opened the door for him. He looked as gorgeous as the night I met him. We arrived at the Biltmore Hotel twenty minutes later.

The hotel sits in a beautiful and affluent community called Coral Gables. The hotel dates back to the early 1900's. Its grandiose appearance makes the hotel a landmark in the city of Coral Gables. The lobby and reception area are decorated with antique furniture from the 18 century. As you glance upward to the ceiling, you notice elaborate frescos covering every square inch of ceiling plaster. Draping over the enormous walls, French and Italian tapestries illustrating peaceful garden scenes with a Victorian glamour taking you back in time when Ballroom dancing was the custom and fashion. The exterior of the hotel has as much charm and elegance as the interior. Several Italian statues that create a path of tranquility and a sense of the Roman Bath era guide you to the swimming pool. The true beauty is the golf course behind the magnificent hotel. It is a well-manicured golf course surrounded by large Ficus and Oak tress with several walking trails that intertwine through the forested golf course.

Small marble benches below the canopy of trees invite walkers to sit and hear the whistling breeze while taking a short respite from their stroll.

I took Victor toward the upstairs bar where he ordered a glass of wine and I ordered a glass of soda. I suggested taking the drinks toward the pool area. We walked alongside the edge of the pool as it curved and twisted in an abstract pond design. I then guided him to the golf course where we continued our romantic stroll. We saw a bench below a large Ficus tree and decided to sit and relax for several minutes. We sat quietly smiling and looking at each other. It was the most precious time to share our first kiss. Gradually, I put my arm around him and moved him closer to me. Moments later, I kissed him. It was a wonderful kiss. One kiss led to another and then another.

Chapter Thirteen

The evening with Victor was enchanting. It appeared that I had met the man that truly made me happy. After our long and romantic stroll through the golf course, we agreed for a late night dinner. He suggested Sushi. Raw fish was a delicatessen that I was not too fond of nor enjoyed. However, I wanted to please him and decided to possess as much enthusiasm as he did regarding the Sushi dinner.

We decided to order take-out and eat it at my apartment. I had no idea what to order and left the decision up to him. He ordered what appeared to be enough food to feed the Japanese army. Actually, it was ten Styrofoam boxes of Japanese Sushi simply to feed two men. We arrived at my apartment where we ate the raw fish while watching television. Not surprisingly, we couldn't eat the entire order and saved the remaining five white containers in the refrigerator. We continued to watch television with intermittent breaks for kissing. It wasn't long before I turned the television off and the main entertainment was the kissing. We continued to kiss passionately for endless hours. It was an evening that I would never forget. At about three in the morning, I told him that it was getting late and I should take him home. He agreed and I drove him to his secret place.

We saw each other quite often the following week. He would come over my place and we would rent movies or we would drive to the beach where we would walk for hours on the moist sandy shore. Our initial dates were never costly. They were rather inexpensive, but wonderful nonetheless. He seemed as excited as I was, but by the end of our first week something happened. He took an emotional nosedive. I am too keen about people's behavior not to recognize that something was wrong. The issue on his mind was my daughter.

I called Victor one evening after he had canceled a date. I told him that I perceived something was wrong, but didn't know what was the matter. After much probing and several moments of uncomfortable silence on the telephone, I decided to say good-bye. Before hanging up, I asked him for a minute of his time. I knew what his issue and problem were about, but wanted him to tell me. Unfortunately, he was too afraid to express his feelings and I then took the initiative to begin speaking about the disturbing topic. He agreed on granting me a minute of his time and I continued to say, "Vic, I have a daughter which is the MOST important part of my life. I would love to share my life and that of my daughter's with someone that can appreciate and understand this love. If you cannot or will not be able to tolerate this situation, I respect you and can only wish you luck in finding a man that is as good as you." He remained silent and then I told him that it was nice knowing him, but there was no need to continue dating. A soft goodnight was said and then we hung up the telephone.

I was sure he would never call again. I underestimated him. The next day late in the afternoon, I received a call at my office from Victor. He apparently reconsidered the decision on not pursuing our relationship further. I was rather surprised by his quick change of heart and told him that I still had a daughter and my life had not changed in the last twenty-four hours. He chuckled and expressed his desire to meet Alexa Rae one day. We continued our dating, but I refused to introduce Alexa Rae to him for quite some time.

Meanwhile, I was still having casual sexual encounters with several men while dating Victor. Victor and I hadn't had sex and therefore I didn't feel obliged to solely exclude myself from any extracurricular activities with other men. Therefore, I continued to have fun with as many boys as I could. My life was becoming difficult to juggle and slowly I began to eliminate the other men from my life. The last one to go was Chad. He was the butch, hairy diesel mechanic. It was certainly a pity letting him go.

Victor and I continued to romantically date for several weeks. Our dates would usually terminate in my apartment watching television and sipping a glass of wine while engaging in passionate kissing. It was a heavenly feeling to spend time with Victor without the sexual intimacy. We did nothing except kiss. No sucking nipples or sucking dicks, it was only kissing. Granted, I was getting off with other men; therefore, it was easy for me to hold back. Actually, we held back for three weeks from the day we met.

My emotions were developing stronger for Victor and I needed to do something about Chad. I didn't want to see him go, but I knew that I wanted to pursue my relationship with Victor monogamously. I called Chad and invited him over my apartment to talk. Despite my intentions, we did very little talking and had many hours of fucking. Chad definitely left with a bang that evening. He arrived wearing a white tank top and loose fitting cargo shorts. He greeted me with a peck on the lips and entered my apartment. After closing the door, he pulled down his shorts unveiling his stiff cock. He bent over and held open his butt cheeks revealing his beckoning hairy hole. I knew then my talk would have to wait until after I fucked him. I went toward his man pussy and began to smother my face deep into his man hole. I lubed it well with spit and began to finger his anus. Gently opening it wider, I inserted one then two and finally my entire fist went inside him. This continued for several long minutes until I was almost ready to burst my load. I instructed him to squeeze his anal sphincter slowly expelling my fist out of his man tunnel. He then went into the bedroom to continue the sexual marathon. When I entered my bedroom, Chad was in his traditional missionary position. His thick hairy legs were spread open and deep inside his hole a nine-inch dildo. I watched as he buried the thick plastic cock inside and then pushed it out unmasking a black hole surrounded by a carpet of dark wet ass hairs. I held his legs wide open by his ankles and instructed him to arch his back giving me easy entry into his man pussy. I began to pound him. Harder and harder, I pounded his ass until he was panting like a wild animal. I reached for the dildo and began to double penetrate him. I dug the plastic dick deep inside him while burrowing my own member deeper into his body. I then began to see his flaccid dick ooze the customary *cum* while feeling his ass muscles tighten around my own dick. I sat over his hairy man chest and began to stroke my cock. I squeezed his mouth open and made him taste my *cum* and shit-coated dick. What an evening! After getting showered and dressed, I did manage to have a short talk with him. I basically told him that I wanted to commit myself to one man and that man was not him. He was understandably upset, but accepted my decision. I have never spoken to Chad, the diesel mechanic, ever again.

The following day was Thanksgiving Day, November 25, 1999. After much hesitation on my part, I invited Victor to have dinner with my family. It had been awhile since I brought someone home to my parents, but they were very welcoming. Victor's ethnic background is Colombian. Traditionally, Colombians are quiet and reserved compared to their Cuban counterparts, which are loud and extremely friendly. We managed to have a wonderful dinner that evening and it was my understanding that Victor enjoyed meeting my entire family as well. We drove back to my apartment where I invited him for a nightcap. I poured him a glass of white wine and myself a glass of apple juice and began to recount the evening at my parents. We laughed and giggled at the dynamics of my slightly *nutty* family and then there was a moment of silence. The moment I had waited to kiss his lips. We began to kiss passionately on the sofa. This time things were getting more sexual. I felt his urge and need to be intimate. I felt his yearning to have sex. I began to unbutton his dress shirt revealing a small patch of chest hair and began to suckle on his large blackened nipples. From his nipples, I went further down cat licking the sides of his tummy and then tongued his belly button. My arm was resting on his crotch and could feel the stiffness of his jeans as his dick was getting larger and harder. I slowly moved my hands from his tummy to the buttons on his jeans and began to unlatch them. I moved my hands over his crispy white Jockey underwear and began to massage the large lump of manhood that was throbbing for pleasure. Casually, garment by garment were being removed exposing our naked bodies to each other. The kissing and fondling continued until we were perspiring profusely. I held his hand

and led him to the bedroom where the fun continued. Every inch of his body was touched and explored while he laid on my bed motionless. I continued to lick him all over as he quietly moaned from the pleasure I was giving him. I wanted nothing in return except to hear him moan louder from the pleasure I was giving his sex hungry body. I savored his body as it was my after dinner dessert. Gradually, I went down to his dick and began to suck on the large mushroom head then I licked the thick shaft of his throbbing penis. Moving downward to his sperm sac, I held both balls in my mouth giving him a warm wet sensation that caused him to squirm from the pleasure. Then, I moved to the space between his ass and his balls and licked the path of course hair while he opened his legs wider and wider allowing my face to sink deeper into his ass. Finally, I got to his tight and beautiful furry hole. I opened his legs slightly giving me a better view of his ass and began to lick his hole as if it was ice cream. He tasted better than the Hagen Daz flavor of the month. I inserted my middle finger into his rectum and began to gently massage his prostate while kissing his lips. Continually, I massaged the pea-like structure until it swelled large and became hardened. I felt his gland pulsate from the excitement that I was producing and began to suck his dick a second time. It wasn't long before his thick, white *cum* spurt inside my mouth. His man juice was sweet honey to my taste buds.

Our relationship began to rapidly grow. He would visit me daily and spend the nights cuddled next to me while we slept. It wasn't long before I emptied a drawer for his stuff and gave him half the closet. He would only sleep once or twice a week in his secret apartment. I still hadn't seen his apartment and I was becoming more curious and weary about his residence. Finally, I asked him what was the mystery about his apartment. The mysterious issue was that he didn't live alone. He shared an apartment with his aunt and uncle that were unaware of his homosexuality. Nonetheless, we continued to have wonderful days together and incredible evenings sharing our bodies intimately.

Several days after meeting Victor, I told him that I was taking my daughter to Disney World and had invited Maybelle to come along with us. It was the first time my daughter would visit the Magic Kingdom and I felt that her Mother would greatly enjoy her daughter's facial expression as she saw Mickey, Minnie and all the other Disney characters. Maybelle and I also made plans to continue our vacation north and visit Stone Mountain in Georgia. I know that Victor was not happy with my vacation plans with Maybelle, but it was too soon in our relationship for him to make any remarks or demands. Having total trust in him, I allowed Victor to stay in my apartment for the seven days I was traveling with Maybelle and Alexa Rae.

I arrived at Maybelle's home early morning on December 2, 1999 (a day after my daughter's birthday) with a rented Sport Utility Vehicle, my luggage and a lack of enthusiasm for our pseudo family vacation. We stuffed the family vehicle with all our belongings and headed north to Orlando, Florida for our Disney World vacation. The four-hour trip felt endless. While Alexa Rae slept in the back seat, Maybelle would only remind me of the pain I had caused her. The one sided conversation continued until we reached the theme park. I was already exhausted and it was only four hours into our vacation.

Our first day at Disney World was spent inside the Magic Kingdom. Maybelle and I did everything possible for Alexa Rae to enjoy her magical vacation with her parents. We enjoyed Alexa Rae's happiness as Mickey, Minnie, Pluto and Donald Duck signed her Disney character autograph book. Meanwhile, Maybelle and I were emotionally exhausted at the effort we needed to put forth in having a wonderful time together. It was especially difficult for her when I would use my cell phone to call Victor. At one instance, Maybelle asked me to call (him) when she was not present or near me. I did as she asked. I would wait until she was inside a store or needed to use the rest room when I would call Victor. We arrived late to our hotel. Maybelle, Alexa Rae and I dropped like flies on the beds. Hotel accommodations in Disney and Stone Mountain were made with two double beds preventing the possibilities of any uncomfortable circumstances for Maybelle or myself. The following day we decided to visit the Animal Kingdom. It is a theme park in the form of a large zoo where kids can enjoy safari rides and learn about various animals and their habitats. Animal Kingdom is much like a city zoo, but in greater magnitude. Alexa Rae was tired from the previous day at the Magic Kingdom and was a bit cranky. We managed to see the entire park and returned to the hotel early evening where we had pizza and coke, as Alexa Rae wanted. After eating our pizza, we entertained Alexa Rae with a painting art set I had purchased in the Animal Kingdom. When she finally fell asleep, Maybelle and I began to pack our suitcases for the twelve-hour road trip to Stone Mountain, Georgia the following morning.

We woke up early and I began storing the luggage pieces into the family vehicle. Then, still fast asleep, I put Alexa Rae into her car seat. We began our journey northward to Georgia. Maybelle and Alexa Rae slept most of the way, which allowed me to have a very relaxing twelve-hour trip. We arrived in Georgia late in the evening giving us little time to enjoy the wonders of Stone Mountain.

The next morning we were well rested and began our Stone Mountain vacation. We climbed the large stone hill and admired the beautiful view from above. Alexa was in awe at how high we had climbed. She kept asking me, "Am I in heaven?" My daughter couldn't believe she was standing on the top of a mountain. We walked and admired the 360-degree view of Stone Mountain while taking small breaks for memorable "family" pictures. After exploring the mountain, we ventured into the nearby forest where we discovered many hidden treasures. Plantation homes, old mills, covered bridges, flowing streams and small waterfalls were some of the hidden prizes we came across.

After our exhausting day, we headed back to the inn where we bathed and dressed for an early dinner. The restaurant was decorated with a considerable amount of charm giving me a sense of warmth. After dinner, we returned to our room for some relaxation and sleep. Maybelle and Alexa

Rae fell asleep quickly and I soon followed. The next day, we spent hours sightseeing the nearby towns and did some shopping at the local craft shops. We arrived late at the hotel and neither one of us were in the mood to dress for dinner. I drove to McDonald's and ordered a *Happy Meal* for Alexa Rae and several hamburgers for Maybelle and I. The third and final day at Stone Mountain were to be spent in a Christmas festival that was being hosted by the town of Stone Mountain.

The Christmas Festival was an all day affair. There was a two hour train ride with Christmas carolers, Santa's home in the forest, various small production plays for children, hot apple cider and many country craft shops. I was strolling through the masses of families saddened by our own family situation. It was heartbreaking to see Maybelle and I as we were acting out the character roles of husband and wife. It was disturbing acknowledging that behind every smile and laughter there was pain and sorrow within us.

We returned to the hotel room tired and decided to pack in the morning. Maybelle showered first and I lay down with Alexa Rae watching television. It wasn't long before I heard the soft snore indicating she was asleep. After my warm shower, I laid in bed. Shortly thereafter, I quietly fell asleep. It must have been an hour or so into my sleep when Maybelle awakened me. Her hand was inside my underwear fondling my semi hard dick. It didn't take long for the semi erection to become solidified. I slowly took her hand out of my boxer shorts and softly told her "NO." My rejection was not because I didn't want to fuck her, but because I didn't want to be unfaithful to Victor. I could have fucked her, but I chose not to confuse her (or myself). I have never had a problem fucking women, but my *gayness* was not simply about sex. My homosexuality was about whom I had become not simply that I wanted to have sex with men. I saw the tears in her eyes as she stood and her lifeless body went back to her bed.

Reality began to hit home as we headed southbound to Miami. Maybelle was beginning to realize that the pseudo family would soon come to an end and that I would return to my homosexual life. She was obviously emotionally upset and short tempered throughout the entire road trip. I arrived at her home and began to unload the suitcases and shopping bags. Moments later, I said good-bye to Maybelle and Alexa Rae and began my drive home to Victor.

As I opened my apartment door, the sweet smell of roses awakened my tired body from the taxing vacation. There were roses everywhere. Red, yellow and white petals flooded every room of the apartment. I was glad to be home.

Christmas was just around the corner and Victor had persuaded me to put up a Christmas tree in my apartment. It would be the first time since my separation from Maybelle that I would decorate and trim a tree for the holidays. Victor and I drove to a nearby Christmas tree lot and searched out the perfect tree for my apartment. It was a six-foot Frasier Fir dense with the fragrance of Christmas pouring through all the needles of its branches. After we had carefully placed the tree inside my small convertible Mazda Miata, we drove home and began to enjoy the trimming of our first Christmas tree.

More than a year has gone by and I am still sharing my life with the same wonderful man. It hasn't been easy, but it has most certainly been rewarding to find Victor amidst all my pain, sorrow and despair. He has anchored me like no one else has done. He has shown me love that I have never fathom existed between two men. I am still learning from him and will continue to learn from the teachings he demonstrates daily.

It was several months after dating Victor that I decided to introduce my daughter to him. I invited him to meet Alexa Rae and myself at her karate class early Saturday morning. He arrived before we did and appeared to be anxious. After her karate, Victor invited us to ice cream and Alexa Rae accepted the offer. She was shy and distant, but soon began to warm up to her daddy's new friend. After several meetings and encounters, Alexa Rae was more accepting of Victor and he seemed more comfortable with his new stepdaughter. It didn't take long before I too felt comfortable incorporating Victor into our outings. My relationship with Victor continued to grow; however, his jealousy and possessive behavior were causing me much discomfort.

Victor was an extremely jealous person and would demonstrate his insecurities constantly. He would monitor every move, telephone call and would tell me how and what to wear when going out. His obsession and jealousy were "cute" at first, but then it became a nuisance. I was afraid of every move I made. I was afraid of making him upset or angry. His insecurities were becoming more of a problem in our relationship and one evening I decided to have a talk with him. My conversation was to tell him I needed a break. I suggested a permanent separation. I couldn't continue our relationship. I began to resent him and I wanted my own space to breathe without someone watching every move I made or suspicious of everything I did. I felt suffocated by him. Fortunately, I had a clear conscience of my faithfulness in our relationship, which made me more upset and angry at the lack of confidence and trust he demonstrated towards me. The separation occurred in our fourth or fifth month of our relationship. I simply asked him to leave my apartment with as many of his personal belongings as he could stuff into his vehicle. He left that spring evening with five trash bags stuffed with clothes, shoes and other personal belonging. I slept wonderfully that evening.

He called my office the following day, but I had instructed my secretary not to transfer any personal calls to me or interrupt me if Victor would happen to call. At home, he had left several messages that went unanswered. It wasn't until the following evening that Victor reached me at home. I was relaxing watching television when he interrupted my *Will and Grace* sitcom. We spoke for several minutes and then he asked me when we would see each other again. He explained to me that he called several therapists and was in the process in making an appointment to begin counseling for his problem. Unfortunately, I wasn't interested in neither continuing my relationship nor giving him a second chance. However, I did recognize his efforts and decided to reconsider my decision. We began to speak on the telephone daily, but I would not make any suggestions to meet. It wasn't until the third week that I asked him out on a dinner date and he agreed.

I made reservations at a nice romantic restaurant in South Beach where we enjoyed each other's company as if it were our first date. After dinner, we walked to a small playhouse and enjoyed a small play. Our evening was spectacular. I didn't want our date to end. I didn't want him sleeping at his aunt's apartment. I wanted him to stay that evening with me. I was falling in love with this man and didn't even know it. I invited him upstairs to my apartment and he did spent the evening with me.

During our separation, I went out once to a dance bar. I met a man while I was dancing. He was gorgeous. He was in his late thirties with salt and pepper hair. He was *cruising* me all night until finally he approached me, as I walked toward the back patio bar. His shirt was opened revealing his hairy chest and his jeans were tight around his round ass. We spoke for several minutes and then I asked him to dance. We danced several songs and before I knew it I was tongue kissing him on the dance floor. After several songs, I needed a rest and decided to go outside with Derick. We walked to his car where the kissing continued and then he began to unbutton my jeans. His large hands reached inside my Calvin Klein underwear were he massaged my hard dick. We continued to kiss and he continued to manipulate my meat. Despite my arousal, it wasn't feeling right. I didn't want Derick. I wanted Victor instead. I gently guided Derick's hand away from my crotch and told him that I wanted to go home. He gave me his telephone number which I later threw out of the car window on my way home and never saw him again.

It didn't take long before Victor had moved his personal belonging back to the bottom drawer of my dresser. The other half of the closet was jammed with his dress shirts and dress pants as well. Our relationship seemed better. He had continued his therapy sessions and apparently the counseling had created a new person. He was a changed man. Gradually, our relationship grew stronger and we began to make plans for our first vacation together. We researched several destinations and agreed on

London and Paris. A trip that Maybelle and I always dreamed about. It was ironic that I would make the trip with my male lover instead of Maybelle. Life tends to be ironic sometimes.

Victor became an integral part of my family. He would accompany me to family birthdays, family dinners and all other family gatherings. It wasn't long before my parents fell in love with Victor. Actually, my family fell in love with him sooner than I. Alexa Rae also became very fond of Victor. She would draw pictures, make cards and call him on the telephone to say "hello." When she would see him, she would run and leap towards his arms while smothering him with kisses. I remember, not too long ago, Victor was holding Alexa Rae in his arms when she held his face with her small hands and gave him a kiss on the cheek. After her demonstration of affection, she said, "I love you." A myriad of emotions ran through my veins like racecars on a speedway. I said nothing and continued as if I heard nothing as well. Later that evening, Victor mentioned the incident to me and I simply smiled acknowledging his comment about my daughter's demonstration of love.

We continued to plan our romantic trip to Europe with enthusiasm. I had less enthusiasm than he about our vacation, but I was still excited about our overseas adventure. We scheduled our trip for September 2000 with our first stop being London, England. We would stay in London for five days and then via the *Euro Train* arrive in Paris for the remainder of our vacation.

I recall a friend asking me several days before departure how I felt about my romantic trip to Europe with Victor. Well, the question opened a can of worms. I expressed that it had always been my dream to visit London and Paris with Maybelle. I wanted to stroll the narrow streets of London holding her hand. I wanted to sit and converse in a cafe overlooking the Eiffel Tower with her. I had dreamed about having a picnic sitting on the lawn of the Champs de Mars. I wanted to feel love in Paris. I wanted to have beautiful and lasting memories of such a dream vacation with the person I loved and cherished. Much to my amazement, my romantic dream vacation was shared with Victor. It is still difficult to let go of Maybelle and it is more difficult to let go of all the dreams we had together. Presently, I have a new life with Victor and I must tell myself that I have new dreams to pursue and accomplish.

I remember being excited and saddened the day I boarded the aircraft to London. Excited that I was traveling overseas to a place I had dreamed about for so long, but saddened that this dream was supposed to be shared with Maybelle. Despite my roller coaster of emotions, I masqueraded my emotions and showed Victor a facade of happiness and enthusiasm. I didn't want his vacation to be ruined by my own issues. I wanted him to have a wonderful time in one of the most romantic parts of the world. Much to my surprise, I soon forgot about the sadness in leaving Maybelle behind and began to fully and completely enjoy the vacation with Victor.

We would wake up early and not arrive back to the hotel until after midnight. We wanted to experience as much as we could in as little time as possible. We visited everything and did everything that we wanted to do and experience. It was not a relaxing vacation considering the miles of walking we did throughout London and then Paris.

I felt something happen to me on the trip. My emotions toward Victor began to change. I would look at him and feel my heart beat at a faster pace. I felt butterflies in my stomach as we walked through the dark streets of London taking pictures of Big Ben and Westminster Abbey. It was the first time I found myself laughing, giggling and enjoying myself with someone other than Maybelle. The very first time since my separation that another person became my best friend. I realized that I was falling in love with Victor in England. We both enjoyed London much more than Paris, but both cities have wonderful lasting memories in our hearts. London is where I fell in love and Paris is where I married the man of my dreams.

We bought matching Cartier rings in Paris and visited Notre Dame Cathedral early the next day where we exchanged vows. Privately, we exchanged our vows and then placed the gold symbol of trust and love around our fingers. We kissed and lit a small candle and then asked a woman tourist to take a picture of both of us on our wedding day. We were married September 9, 2000. We had known each other now for almost one year. We felt proud and accomplished at how many obstacles we had jumped over and how many more we had to face. We felt we were partners for life.

We arrived back to Miami exhausted and carrying more luggage than we had taken to Europe initially. We shopped everywhere and bought almost everything. One of the many things we purchased was our first pillbox. We bought a beautiful pillbox in London and decided to begin a collection together. It was our first collection as a couple. Today, we have six porcelain pillboxes from our travels. We bought suits, jackets, shoes and anything that we felt we couldn't find in the U.S. or simply wanted to tell our friends, "We bought this in Paris." It certainly was a beautiful trip with enchanting memories.

Our next trip was a milestone for both Victor and I (and Maybelle as well). For Alexa Rae's birthday in December, I made plans to take her to Disney World for her second visit. The difference this time was that Maybelle was not invited. It was a turning point in my life, Maybelle's life and Victor's life. It was a trip that I carefully thought about and concluded that my partner, Victor, was whom I wanted to invite. I also invited Carlie, a friend of Alexa Rae. Maybelle did not agree to the Disney trip easily. Her issue was not about my homosexuality nor my lover, but about not letting go of her husband and her family. She wanted to be Victor. She wanted to have my love. She wanted to be a family again. Nonetheless, Alexa Rae had a wonderful time. We visited as many parks and attractions as our time allotted and then the weekend came to an end. We had to leave fantasyland behind and return to reality.

It has been more than one year with my wonderful husband and I am still as happy as the day I met him at Splash. I still have many issues about commitment and with time I feel confident that all my issues will be resolved. One of my issues is to unite finances and mutually own property. Victor has in several occasions mentioned to purchase a house together. I simply ignored his comments or would tell him, "One day, hon." He is in the process of purchasing an automobile and wants to include my name on the title of the vehicle. I wish he wouldn't. A year ago, we decided to place pocket change into a large glass container. The plan (his plan, not mine) was to fill the container with coins and open a mutual savings account. The container was filled to the brim with coins, but I simply began to pour my pocket change into another glass container. This container is larger and hopefully will take longer to fill with our pocket change. He mentioned several weeks ago about counting the change and taking the rolled coins to the bank; however, I simply said, "One day, hon." I am just not ready to go beyond where I am now. The act of buying a house, purchasing a vehicle or opening a bank account together creates an eternal commitment to each other. I am not ready to be in such a relationship. I am still not emotionally or eternally committed to him. I am afraid. I am fearful that he might find someone that is better looking, younger, more affectionate or simply someone new. However, these are my own insecurities, but deep down inside I know that Victor loves me. Even though it terrifies me to buy a home or simply open a bank account, I am looking forward to that day with him.

I don't know who will take care of me when I am sick or hold my hand when I am dying. I don't know what will happen tomorrow or next week, so I simply take it one day at a time. He seems to be a wonderful man today and that is what's important for me now. He is the only man that has made me laugh. The only one.

Chapter Fourteen

It has been five long years traveling through my life. A journey that allowed me to emotionally grow, seek out my true identity and given me strong values and personal integrity. However, the same journey has given me many sorrowful days and nights. The choices I've made in leaving my wife and family will continue to reek havoc my entire life, but it has allowed me to live a truthful life without lies or adultery. The choices I made to prostitute my body will forever haunt me with my partner, but it made me understand the difference between love and sex. The choice I made to "come out" will have consequences tomorrow, but it has allowed me to feel pride for the first time in my life. All our conscience choices have consequences. Every choice I made has had both good and bad consequences.

The hardest choice I've made was abandoning my daughter. I left Alexa Rae behind to become whole and complete as a man. I abandoned her to become a homosexual man. I left her behind for her to one day tell me that I was a man of truth, honor and value. I wanted to teach her that life without truth, honor and values is not a life worth living. Through my mistakes, I have learned the true path in life. Today, my daughter can learn from me and travel her Life Journey without the horrors and terrors I once faced in my own path.

Every gay father can relate with the sadness we awaken to on holidays. It is an emptiness in our hearts that no one can fill. It is a void with only sorrow lingering through the blackness of matter. Holidays should be joyous, but instead it becomes a pulsating pain traveling through our veins that no one can alleviate or comfort. Every Halloween night that I can't see my daughter's costume is a dagger through my spleen. Every Thanksgiving dinner that I don't sit next to my angel is a sword through my liver. And, every Christmas morning that I don't see my Princess' eyes when she awakens is a lance through my heart. Holidays kill me. I miss my daughter every moment and every second of the day. I yearn for her every day of the year. I pray that she forgives me.

Every day is a new challenge for me. Upon daybreak, my mind begins to wonder about my choices, my daughter and the pain I have caused the people I love so dearly. It has been five years and still not a day goes by that the pain has gone away. The pain lingers everyday as an incurable fatal cancer that prevents happiness and joy to reach my heart. It is a parasite that harbors and invades my body eating slowly at my soul. Everyday I ask myself, *Why is this lifestyle so difficult? Why so much pain? Why so much sorrow?* I have concluded that there are as many variables making the gay lifestyle difficult, as there are leaves on an Oak tree. When we enter the gay world we encounter a new life. The gay life is not only foreign to many of us, but has rules that are not familiar to many of us. As a gay man, we learn to deal with deep issues that no straight man has ever dealt with. Sometimes, our sorrows, pains, despair and past issues surface without warnings throughout our lives. As gay men, we learn to deal with the prejudices of society, friends and family. We taste rejection from our parents and even children. We learn to love a person of the same sex. As a gay couple, we learn how to share our lives, homes and finances without a legal marriage. As a gay male, we learn the necessity to keep ourselves in decent bodily shape, if we want a boyfriend. We learn how to *cruise* and be *cruised* in a bar. And for God's sakes, we even learn to eat foods high in fiber and douche regularly before sexual intercourse. It is a lifelong learning experience that most of us begin later in life and never master. Today, I realize why so many gay men have not mastered the happiness and joy gay life can bring them.

My relationship with Victor hasn't been all peaches and honey, but neither was my marriage to Maybelle though I fell madly and passionately in love nonetheless. No relationship will ever be perfect. With patience, I am hopeful that I will arrive at that love once again. Victor and I have had our share of ups and downs, but we have managed to keep our relationship together. Actually, he has been the one that hasn't run away. I appreciate his patience, struggles and the love he has demonstrated me. I have realized that he is my Prince. He is a man that any man (gay) would dream of having. He is pleasant and loving, nurturing and sweet. He is what Maybelle was and probably more-a MAN. Yet, I still say "good night" to her in my dreams.

I remember a telephone conversation I recently had with Maybelle. She asked me if I was happy. I couldn't answer her quickly and due to my delay she gathered I was not completely happy. Her assumption was correct. She too expressed her unhappiness despite her many casual dates. She began to tell me about the men in her life. It became uncomfortable to say the least. According to her, all the men seemed to be quality individuals. "They all have good careers and are emotionally capable and ready to be in caring and loving relationship", she remarked. I asked if her plans were to settle down with one of these men and establish a long-term committed relationship. She said, "NO!" It seems to me that she suffers from the same pain as I do. The pain caused by not letting go of our pasts. She continued to tell me how handsome these men were and how sexy they made her feel. She went on further and expressed that for the first time she has felt like a woman that is yearned and wanted by men. Maybelle continued her illustrative description on how these men touched her, kissed her and made love to her while I listened without interruptions. Once she finished her erotic storytelling, I told her how interesting that our divorce allowed both of us to find something we were missing in our relationship. With my treasured search for man sex, I found emptiness and loneliness. I left my family to feel complete and whole, but I found myself more incomplete then before. Maybelle found her womanhood, but lost love. We both gained and we both lost something.

I ask myself, *Does simply sucking dick and fucking a man make another man gay? Is there more in being gay than gay sex? Can I be married to a woman and have sex with men and be content? Can I or will I be happy in a heterosexual marriage? Can I or will I be happy in a gay marriage?* I don't know. I wish I had all the answers, but I don't. What I do know from my research and my personal experiences is that a person's sexuality and a person's lifestyle are two different animals. Living a lifestyle (whether gay or straight) is a choice. A conscience decision we make to share a life or live a life, as we want to live. However, being gay is not a choice, but our most integral part of our persona. In other words, we can be gay, but make a conscience choice to live a straight or gay lifestyle. However, we don't have a choice to be straight if we are gay. God created our *gayness* or *straightness* and we have no choice to accept the gift with happiness and gratitude. God made us to be happy with the life he chose for us; therefore, family, friends or society should not prevent us from arriving at our happiness by delegating how or with whom we should share our lives. I was born gay and gay I will be until the day I die regardless of what or whom I want to be. I am and will always be a gay man. In my own life experiences, I found it difficult to be a gay man and live a straight life causing an insurmountable amount of pain and anguish. Uniting my sexuality with my lifestyle has allowed me completeness and wholeness as a human being. Nonetheless, this doesn't mean that my choices or decisions are best for everyone. Every gay man needs to carefully search for his own happiness in life. Whether their happiness is to live a straight life or gay lifestyle is not important. The important issue to remember is to fully accept whom you are regardless of where and how you have chosen to live your life.

Being gay doesn't mean you can't or won't fall in love with a woman. I did. *Gayness* has nothing do to with whom we chose to love or whom we want to share our lives. *Gay* is an identity. I fell in love with Maybelle because of her qualities not her body. I fell in love with her smile and her touch. I fell in love with her inner beauty and how that beauty radiated outward to shine on me. Ironically, all this love was not enough to keep me married to her. I needed to search for something else. MEN. It is ironic that I could not or would not put aside the sexual pleasures of man sex and create a deeper relationship based not on sex, but love with

Maybelle. It was my choice. A choice I made to leave my marriage and child to find wholeness and completeness with a man. My picture perfect life became a melting pot of grief, pain, and discomfort.

It has been five years since my journey began. My daughter speaks in full sentences and has started Kindergarten. My ex-wife has built a beautiful two-story home. She has restarted her life and seems to be on her way to earning her doctorate degree. My parents have supported and accepted their gay son. My friends seem to accept me for who I am. My career seems to be moving forward. I've managed to rebuild my life in a new setting and purchased a small apartment close to my office. I appear to be happier than yesterday and hopefully will be less unhappy today then tomorrow. Through my journey, I have gain insight and wisdom. I have learned to love myself and share the love I have with others. Occasionally as the world appears dynamic and in constant motion, it sometimes becomes difficult for me to move forward in my own life. Yet, I continue to move.

Occasionally, in the darkness of night, I sit on my balcony wondering what thoughts and feelings tomorrow will bring. I reflect on my life and feel proud of what I've accomplished and sad at the pain I've suffered getting here. As I sit on my white wicker balcony chair, I pray for my daughter's forgiveness. I wonder what she dreams about and how she's sleeping. I glance over to the side of the balcony and notice Alexa Rae's bicycle. It is a small pink bike with a white basket and training wheels that she has never ridden. Yet, I still hold on to the iron relic hoping that one day I can see her ride it. I look over across my building toward the adjacent six story edifice and notice people turning off their bedroom lights. I ask myself, *Are they alone? Are they sad and unhappy? Are they holding on to someone they love?* My mind ponders and wonders about what keeps people going. What makes these individuals wake up in the mornings? Then, passive thoughts of suicide enter my mind and I want to jump over the iron bars. I don't. I am not a quitter and will continue to strive for personal and eternal happiness in my life. Lights flicker off as people close their eyes. I wonder who they will hold and cuddle for warmth. Momentarily, my thoughts are rambled by the noise the airplanes jets make overhead. Then, I continue to ponder about my life.

Inside my apartment, awaits my husband in bed. He is asleep and does-n't know my thoughts or feelings or why my happiness is sometimes masked by sadness and misery. I wonder how long he can love a man with so many torments and pains. How long can he wait before I commit my love to him?

For ten years of my life, I held Maybelle in my arms to sleep. Cuddling and spooning each other for warmth, security and as a demonstration of our love, we held each other all night long. Together we dreamed and held each other tightly during our sleep. Today, I cuddle with a man. As I put my arms around him, I feel the strength of his manhood and the power of his body. Something happens in the midst of our unconscious sleep. We awaken not holding each other, but our pillows instead. For ten years, I held her in my arms to sleep all night long.

In my own search for answers, I have met many men in similar circum-stances. Many of these men shared similar situations with similar pains and sorrows as me. I have spoken to many married gay men about their lives and situation at home. They have, in many instances, asked me for advice and guidance. I feel empathy for these men as they travel the jour-ney of their lives as I once did. As I listen to their story, I can only tell them to embrace the love they have from their wives and children. I tell them to hold on to their lives while not jeopardizing their sexual identity. I tell them to be gay with pride while making a choice about their lifestyles. I encouraged these confused and hurting men to reflect upon what they have and what they may lose in their choices. Sometimes, the loss outweighs the gain. Other times, the gain outweighs the loss. It is an individual choice. Keep in mind, that my advice is to never jeopardize our sexual identity. We must be truthful and accepting of ourselves regardless of what lifestyle we chose to live. We must love who we are and only then can we be happy loving someone else. I have never encouraged any gay man to leave their wives nor to stay in their marriage. Rather, I have encouraged these men to love themselves as gay men.

I wish that someone had guided me as I have opened the eyes and hearts for many gay married men. The gay life is not for everyone. For some men, the leap into *gayhood* was the best thing that ever happened to their lives. For others, they've leaped into a whirlpool of pain, anguish, sorrow and despair. I will never discourage my gay comrades to take the leap. I did and don't regret it. Nor, will I ever encourage their plunge. In my own search for gay happiness, I left behind my family. I abandoned my wife and child to pursue another life without regards to their emotions or feelings. I left behind true love. A love that was innocent and pure. It was a love that had history and a future. I left behind a dream.

Every morning before arriving at the office, I stop at a local restaurant to have a cup of *cafe con leche* and Cuban toast. While I relax drinking my morning coffee, I write notes in my journal. These short notes become organized into sentences then paragraphs. Finally, from these notes, I created this book.

This morning as I sit sipping my coffee, I begin to reflect one last time on my journey. The journey that has created the man I am today. A road that has been filled with hurt and pain and anguish. Today, I have managed to repave the road into a smooth path where I travel without bumps or obstacles. Deep inside my soul, I can still touch and taste my past and at several moments throughout the day I can still feel the pain. Today the pains, anguish, sorrows, despairs and fears are replaced with a smile as I look back at my life. It is a smile of accomplishment recognizing I have become a wonderful man, father, partner, son and friends to many.

As I take a sip of the coffee, I glance over the table diagonal to where I sit and notice a teen-aged boy surrounded by four girls. He must be thirteen or fourteen years old. He is slender and well groomed with blond highlights in his hair. He wears a loop silver earring and has two or three silver bands around his fingers. As they giggle and converse, I notice that he appears to be effeminate. The movements of his eyes, lips and hands were clear indicators that he was a *sissy*. As he got up from his booth to fetch napkins, I observed his waist swish as mine did when I was his age. As he is walking back to his booth with the napkins in his hand, he looks directly into my eyes. The teenager begins to stare at me while his friends are busy talking. Mesmerized, he stares and I watch as this young boy has lost himself in a fantasy dream world.

This morning I concluded that the cycle of pain and sorrow doesn't end with me. Six feet in front of me sits a boy that will travel my journey. Only this time, it will be HIS journey. I look at this young boy and smile at him with compassion. A smile that illustrates to him he is not alone in this world. I wish that I can hold his hand and guide him through his path, but the road of life is traveled alone. The group of youngsters stands and the boy leaves several bills on the booth table. As the teenage boy grabs his nap sack, I say a prayer for him. I hope God listened.

My own journey in life has led me through many dark and isolate paths and many lakes and rivers of tears. It has taken me many years to arrive at where I am today. A place that I feel secure, peaceful and content. I have reached a place that allows me to look back at my life without fear and sorrow. I've searched long and hard in my Life Journey and finally discovered what I was desperate to find. I have found my HAPPINESS.

About the Author

I love to receive letters and read them all, but I can't promise to respond. If you would like to contact me, please email me at the following: alrod121@aol.com